Profits for Non-Profits:

Running a Successful Non-Profit Gift Shop

ExpandingPress.com
200 West 34th, Suite 953
Anchorage, AK 99503
For orders or questions (281) 419-5122
http://www.giftshopguide.com
info@expandingyourmind.com

Production Manager: Sue Littlepage
Cover Design: Sue Littlepage
Editor: C. Kirk

Copyright © 2005 by Nancy Kirk
Expanding Press
200 West 34th
Suite 953
Anchorage, AK 99503
1-866-313-MIND

DISCLAIMER:

This publication is designed to provide accurate and authoritative information in regard to the subject matter covered. It is sold with the understanding that the publisher is not engaged in rendering professional services. If legal, accounting, medical, psychological or any other expert assistance is required, the services of a competent professional person should be sought.

Every effort has been made to make this a manual as complete and accurate as possible. However, there may be mistakes both typographical and in content. Therefore this text should be used only as a general guide and not as the ultimate source on legal and financial advice on how to run a gift shop. The purpose of this book is to educate and entertain. The author and ExpandingPress and its affiliates shall have neither liability nor responsibility to any person or entity with respect to any loss or damage caused or alleged to have been caused, directly or indirectly, by the information contained in this book.

If you do not wish to be bound by the above and by the copyright laws of the United States, you may

return this book to the publisher for a full refund.

BULK ORDERS? QUESTIONS? NEED HELP?

This book is available at quantity discounts for orders of 10 or more copies.

Email Nancy Kirk, nancykirk@houston.rr.com for pricing and any questions.
Or visit the www.giftShopGuide.com for more information.
ISBN 1-4116-0518-7
Copyright 2005

Profits for Non-Profits:
RUNNING A SUCCESSFUL NON-PROFIT GIFT SHOP

Learn How To:

Plan for Success
Cater to Your Customers
Motivate Volunteers!
Keep Accurate Records
Display Merchandise
Promote Your Gift Shop
Run Things the Right Way!

Perfect For:

Garden Club Volunteers
Museum Shop Directors
Hospital Gift Shop Managers
Any Non-Profit Gift Shop!

Nancy Kirk

Includes Business Forms for Quick Startup!

Dedication

This gift shop guide is dedicated to all the volunteers that give of their time and talents. Their contributions to society are endless!

Volunteers

Valuable is the work you do.

Outstanding is how you always come through.

Loyal, sincere and full of good cheer.

Untiring in your efforts through the year.

Notable are the contributions you make.

Trustworthy in every project you take.

Eager to reach your goals.

Effective in the way you fulfill your role.

Ready with a smile like a shining star.

Special and wonderful-that's what you are.

Insights – Summer 2003

TABLE OF CONTENTS

Introduction

A Note from Nancy

Over the past few years, our economy has seen a dramatic downturn. The change in the world's economy has had an impact on non-profit organizations everywhere. Donations to museums, zoos, hospitals and other such organizations have declined. It's becoming harder to recruit volunteers. Many people that had time to volunteer are now reentering the job market, while corporation donors are becoming far more conservative with their donations as their own profits decline and pressure from stockholders increase. This means, now as never before, non-profit organizations, institutions and facilities have to rely on internal resources to help supplement their causes since funding sources are drying up. And that's where this book comes in.

One of the largest resources for raising money for non-profits, whether it's for the local museum, zoo, hospital or other non-profit organizations, is the gift shop. Gift shops operated by volunteers can aid in supplementing funding loss and even eclipse some other funding sources, if and only if the gift shop is run with an eye towards making a profit. This book is a real-world guide to helping boost sales in these shops.

If you are involved in the operations of a non-profit gift shop, you need to know how to maximize your resources for maximum profitability regardless of whether you employ paid retail management support or work strictly with volunteers. But profitability in a non-profit gift shop? Really?

Yes! What most people don't realize is that that gift shops in a non-profit setting can be money-making businesses.

If any gift shop is to survive in a non-profit setting, **it must be profitable!**

A gift shop run within a non-profit setting really is all about making money, not to put in the pockets of others, but to help fund the hospital, zoo, museum, library or a municipal park. Money made from such shops could go towards buying new state-of-the-art medical equipment, help revamp old exhibits, or add books to library shelves. So right this minute, strike from your mind the misconception gift shops are just to accommodate patrons! This is definitely no longer the case. In many settings the gift shop actually keeps many non-profits going.

And that's what this guide is all about – how to make a profit in a non-profit setting. It's a culmination of my years of experience running profitable gift shops for non-profits. I've included step-by-step instructions on how to get your shop started, and how to make money all the while appreciating and respecting the time and talents of the volunteers that help make the shop a success.

Whether you're a volunteer shop manager, president of a volunteer organization or chairman of the annual bazaar, the information in these pages will be invaluable. It's a step by step guide that includes such daily tools as sample letters, business forms, contracts and illustrations and is compiled from over 30 years experience of running two successful non-profit gift shops, one reinvented from the ground-up. The same techniques used in this book were used:

- In a hospital gift shop I doubled sales and tripled profits in less than a year, allowing the hospital to purchase much needed medical equipment.

- In a municipal garden gift shop on the verge of closing, I showed the city that the little shop could be successful, ending up the year not only profitable, but with enough funds to help in expanding the municipal garden center.

This book will show you how to improve sales and most importantly how to increase profits, whether your shop has volunteer management or a paid staff. You'll gain an understanding of how to select merchandise and marketing unique gift ideas and products, and most importantly, an understanding of why the volunteer is the core of this type of business and how to work with them to maximize your organization's potential using volunteers.

Using a few simple rules and guidelines, any volunteer organization can make their gift shop, bazaar, rummage sale or special event sale, a success.

You do not need the intervention of a large franchise to run your organization. You may not even need to pay a manager to run your gift shop. With a little hard work, some ingenious ideas that you will pick up from this guide and the help of your volunteers, the rewards will be tremendous not only for the gift shop but the volunteer organization.

But you do need one very important piece – volunteers.

The Volunteer – The Core of Your Shop!

Volunteers can be the key to any gift shop's success. The time they contribute is valuable to themselves and to the institution or facility where they offer their services. Without volunteers, most of these shops wouldn't exist. And for many shops, using volunteers is their competitive advantage. So it's imperative you use their time and talent wisely! Because of their value, volunteers are in great demand to staff hospitals, museums, parks, zoos and other non-profit organization's gift shops.

But most non-profit gift shops fail to realize the gold mine they have in the volunteers, and how, if effectively trained and utilized, they can help any gift shop turn a profit. Believe me when I say, dedicated volunteers would rather be working in a shop that is profitable than just "playing store" in a money-loosing venture. The volunteer wants to know that they are making a contribution and with this book you can help them do just that.

As the need to squeeze more dollars out of each donation continues, the volunteer becomes more important. Trends towards paying someone to manage retail non-profit shops are increasingly becoming less cost-effective. In the past, hands-off retail management has been a convenient way for the non-profits to operate a gift shop. But paying a company to run a shop cuts into the profits, ultimately reducing the amount of funds that go back to your organization, which means the responsibility of running the gift shops increasingly falls on the volunteers.

In closing, I'd like to share with you a poem about volunteer motivation. As both a volunteer and former manager, I think this poem captures the essence of what volunteers are all about. If you are a volunteer or work with volunteers, I think you'll agree with the message of this poem. It goes like this…

The Volunteer Viewpoint

By J. Donald Phillips, Hillsdale College
(With permission from "The Envoy", Morristown, NJ)

*"If you want my loyalty, interests, best efforts, remember that:
I need a Sense of Belonging, a feeling that I am honestly needed for
my total self, not just my hands, nor because I take orders well.*

*I need to have a Sense of Sharing in planning our objectives
(my need will be satisfied only when I feel My ideas have had a fair hearing).
I need to feel that my goals and objectives are arrived at are within
reach and that they make sense to Me.*

*I need to feel that what I am doing has a real Purpose or contributes
to human welfare-- that its value extends beyond my personal gain or hours.
I need to know in some clear detail just what is expected of me —
not only my detailed task but where I have the opportunity
to make personal and final decisions.*

*I need to have some responsibilities
that challenge, that are within my assigned goal and contribute to the total goal.*

*I need to See that Progress is being made towards the goals we have set.
I need to be kept informed.*

*What I'm not Up on, I may be Down on
(keeping me informed is one way to give me status as an Individual).*

*I need to have Confidence in my superiors--confidence based on the
Assurance of consistent fair treatment, or recognition when it is due, and
Trust plus loyalty will bring increased security.*

*In brief, no matter how much sense my part in this organization means to You,
I must feel that the whole deal makes sense to Me."*

Chapter 1
First Step: Goals

Goal (goal) n. 1. Something toward which effort or movement is directed; an end or objective.

To be successful you must have goals. With a successful shop, the shop, you and everyone in the shop must have goals, no exception. Don't confuse goals with "To-Do Lists" or yearly resolutions. Many people write down their daily lists of things to do or resolve to do certain things each year, but these are not goals. Goals outline specific accomplishments done in a specific timeframe.

NOTE: If you've never set goals before, a great book on goal setting is Brian Tracy's "Goals! How to Get Everything You Want".

Don't know where to start formulating goals for your shop? A successful shop's goals can be culled from many different sources, from the feedback you get from the customer to actual specifics detailed in manuals, budgets and plans. Here's a quick rundown of where you can look for and where you should establish the goals for your gift shop.

- ✓ In writing the business plan
  (Spelling out exactly the direction the shop should take)
- ✓ In drafting budgets for all expenditures
- ✓ In establishing policies and procedures
- ✓ In compiling an operational manual for the shop
- ✓ In planning of the layout of the shop, (both location and design)
- ✓ In providing customer service
- ✓ In purchasing merchandise to sell in the shop
- ✓ In training a well informed volunteer staff
- ✓ In recognition of the value of the volunteer

Setting goals is not a complicated process nor does it take a lot of time. Using the goal setting techniques listed below will help you achieve your targets. This simple technique will subconsciously suggest to you and those around you that your goals are on the way to achievement and ultimately will become a reality. It will attract the people, places, and situations you need to achieve your goals.

What is the first technique? First, put the goals you want to attain for the shop in writing. This simple act helps you clarify the goals and will allow you to visualize them more effectively. Set goals that will push you beyond what you think you can accomplish. Make sure you include in your goal making process other volunteers that have an interest in the gift shop. Have them take what you've written and add to those goals. This way the goals will become the vision of a group and this will add strength to attaining those goals. Volunteers may also have a better perspective on what goals should be reached because they are not involved in the day to day processes. They will bring a fresh perspective on what can and should be attained.

The second technique is to "present tense" the goals. When listing your goals for the shop phrase each goal in the present tense and then assume success. Instead of writing, "We will achieve $100K in sales," instead write, "We're working toward total sales of $100K. Setting each goal in present tense will help you and your volunteers not look forward to, but realize these goals are things you should be doing today.

The third technique is to set a deadline to accomplish EACH goal. A goal without a deadline is simply a dream. Attach a realistic yet challenging deadline for accomplishing each goal. Don't say, "By next quarter we'll achieve $100K in sales", but rather write "We are working toward sales of $100K and will achieve that by October 15, 2006."

The fourth technique is to list the benefits you intend to receive by achieving each goal. This will keep your group focused when you face the inevitable roadblocks and barriers. Here's an example:

> "We are working toward sales of $100K and will achieve that by October 15, 2006. Once we reach this goal, we will use the profits from these sales to purchase a refrigerated case to display our fresh flowers."

The fifth and final technique is to compile your list of random goals into a finalized form. And for any business, that finalized list of goals is called a business plan. A business plan will help you identify each area of the business that needs specific goals

So let's get started on those goals, by starting with that first step – the business plan. In the next chapter you will be guided, step by step, through all the phases of setting up and operating a gift shop.

Chapter 2
Second Step: The Business Plan

The old adage, "those who fail, fail to plan," couldn't be more applicable than in the retail businesses. Regardless of whether a business is a non-profit run by volunteers or a for-profit business staffed by paid employees, **goals are the most important first step**. The logical next step after setting your goals is to incorporate them into a written business plan. That's exactly what you'll learn how to do in this chapter.

Why Write a Business Plan?

Why write a business plan? What if your shop is a small shop? What if the shop is barely making a profit? What if you do not have many customers? Regardless of your physical size or financial status, you need a plan. When you create a business plan, you are creating a road map of how the business should be run, who is responsible for what, and how to achieve your outlined goals. Your shop also needs a plan if you plan to secure support of any kind, be it monetary or even just the support from a group of volunteers. You will need a plan to convey the shop's purpose, goals, and expectations.

Also a business plan maybe required by the board of your volunteer organization and the institution or facility administration under which it operates. Even if a business plan is not required, the manager of the shop should present one to the administration. This will this show the board and administration that you intend to carry out the operations of the shop in a business-like manner. It will also prevent any miscommunication that could lead to misunderstandings about policies and procedures concerning the shop's operations, not only for the administrative board, but also for those who volunteer.

Finally, a business plan allows you to set goals specifying where you want to be in the future. Almost all successful businesses, regardless of how small when they first started, started with a plan.

Ever heard of McDonald's? That big business started as a small hamburger stand. But as we all know, it is no longer a small business, it's a huge franchise. And why has McDonald's survived when many other small restaurants failed? It lies in the fact that every aspect in McDonald's business, down to the number of pickles they put on your burger has been planned, thought-out and detailed in writing. Visit any McDonald's restaurant, and you can almost see the plan come to life in the uniform way things are done, in the way each workers performs his duty. This is no accident; it's a business plan at work.

McDonald's, succeeded because they set guidelines and followed them, but remained flexible to change plans as their market changed. And this is something you should take note of – any good plan is detailed, yet flexible to allow for changing market conditions.

In addition to a business plan, you'll also need a detailed operations manual. Chapter 5 goes into more detail concerning the Operations manual. Typically where the operation is not complex or is relatively small, the operations manual could even take place of the business plan. The business plan and/or operations manual will outline how the business will operate, creates a roadmap for success, outlines information about markets, customers and procedures and specifies which suppliers the shop will use. The plan, if outlined in a short concise method gives the shop the best chance of succeeding.

Getting Started With a Plan

To get started writing a plan, identify the purpose of the shop, what you want to achieve and your visions for the future of the shop. I found the best way to start any business plan is to write down some major points about your shop and where you see the business will be in the near future. Here's an example of an outline I've used for several shops. I used these and expanded upon them to eventually formulate an operations plan.

The Bare Bones Business Plan:
What we do & our purpose:
- ✓ Sell gift items to those who visit the zoo.
- ✓ Provide education of the wonders and complexity of animal life, and promoting conservation and research.
- ✓ Help promote the zoo thru the gifts and activities we sell/promote

Our target customer is:
Children who visit the zoo

Our big plan for the year:
To raise $50,000 to help build a new petting zoo by November 30, 2006.

Where we are now:
Our sales last year were a little over $86,000.
Profit was $31,000

Projection:
Raise sales to achieve goal of $50,000 profit by November 30, 2006.

See how simple it is? Notice that I've listed what the shop does and what the major plan for the year is. I've identified the target customer and stated our goal for the year. If you have a simple one-two-three list like that, you're ready to really get started.

When I first started, I determined where we were, where we wanted to go, and the customers we catered to. Because the records that had been kept were incomplete, we truly didn't have a clear picture of our real customer. And because we didn't have a big budget for surveys, every time someone purchased something from the shop, we did an informal survey asking why they shopped there, what items they'd like to see, what they thought of our merchandising. Much to our surprise our customer base wasn't just the visitors to the non-profit, but also employees who worked at the organization. Quickly we realized we could cater to a new type of customer we hadn't even realized we were serving.

Since the task of writing an entire plan (and eventually operations manual) may seem daunting, to help you get started, I have included an outline of a business plan later in this chapter. I used this plan for a small hospital shop I managed in Texas. The shop had been in existence for 10 years before I took on the challenge. I started out, first, by figuring out where we were, where we wanted to go, and who we catered to.

From there, with the valuable input from the volunteers and hospital board, we created a plan. Once we had an idea of where we were, we created a plan that opened up our eyes to new opportunities the shop had never before experienced

Before doing this preliminary work, the shop was somewhat floundering, grossing less than $20,000 per year. Although it could make more, it stayed at this level for years mainly because there was no business plan, no operating manual, no budget and most importantly no goals to strive for.

After creating a plan, then sharing it with all the volunteers and the hospital's executive board, everyone quickly understood the potential the shop could reach, and what our actual goals were.

From this plan, a budget and an operating manual quickly emerged. The budget established financial goals and set-up a guideline for effective spending and the manual helped the volunteers understand their roles and responsibilities on a day to day basis, by setting out and defining policies and procedures. Mainly the plan gave everyone the feeling the shop was a business - a business to make money, money that would eventually benefit the hospital.

Believe it or not, after a year using the plan as a roadmap, keeping to the budget and following our operations manual as a day-to-day guide, sales doubled! It was the same gift shop, the same location, the same set of outstanding volunteers, the same hospital we were working to support. A clear, concise plan that gave everyone a vision and goal to shoot for made the difference.

I didn't have a lot money or even time on my hands to create this plan. (At the time I was also volunteering my time in addition to running the shop.) What I did have were a couple of free nights over about two weeks I used to write the plan. I knew if I got it started, working with everyone over a month or so we could quickly refine it, and then put our action plans in place.

Business Plan Resources:

You don't need to run out and buy books on writing a business plan or download any special software. All you need is a word processor, and a simple outline. And I've included the outline on the following pages. You might also take a quick look at some of the free resources on the Internet listed below:

- **Entrepreneur.com**

  Click the link for startups. There are several articles about writing and updating business plans for non-profits.

- **Small Business Administration (www.sba.org)**

  Great resource for free and low-cost seminars as well as offering a lot of online information. Check out http://www.onlinewbc.gov/docs/starting/basics.html for SBA's information on the basics of writing a business plan. Also be sure to check out their non-profit section at http://www.sbaonline.sba.gov/nonprofit/

- **Bplans.com**

  There's a variety of sample business plans you can check out. It also houses a very good list of articles about small business.

- **Businessplans.org**

  Another great place for understanding the business planning process for all sorts of businesses

OUTLINE OF THE BUSINESS PLAN

I.   COVER SHEET
        Pertinent Information
              Name of Shop
              Mission Statement
              Address
              Phone
              Fax
              E-mail/Web site
              Hours

II.   Table of Contents

III.   SUMMARY OF BUSINESS CONCEPTS
        Brief description of the shop
              Current status of shop
                  (Starting out or established)
                      Future projections
              Primary target customer
              Projection of sales volume
        Budget
              $ Needed for operation

IV.   GENERAL PHILOSOPHY
        Principles of running Gift Shop

V.   MARKETING
        Merchandising
        Type of merchandise
        Pricing
        Advertising
        Customer Service

VI.   Management
        Division of responsibilities (Departments)

VII.   Summary of Financial & Operating Statements

VIII.   Manual
              Day to Day Operations (Order of operation)
              Duties of Gift Shop Volunteer
              Policies and Procedures
              Equipment operations instructions

This outline has been compiled especially for a gift shop in a non-profit setting. Most of the business plans you will see in the book stores and on the Internet are specifically written for a regular retail businesses. Even though the object is to make a profit, in both the non-profit and regular retail shop the requirements and objectives are a little different. The printed information available on writing a business plan has to do, mostly, with the financial backing of a new business. The example plans are written just for that purpose. Since you will not need to secure any financing to startup the shop, your goals, of course, are different. That's why I don't recommend spending too much time or money looking at traditional business plan resources.

Filling in the Details

To expand upon the above outline and provide you with the needed details, I suggest following the advice of every good newspaper reporter. Ask the questions, **Who? Where? What? Why? How?** Take each section of the plan and ask these five questions. Answering these questions will be the key to a well-written plan and will help you expand upon issues important to your particular shop. Keep asking yourself these questions as you work toward coming up with definitive goals in each area of the plan.

Form a Committee to Help Write the Plan
Remember the business plan is the guide for the operations of a successful shop, so a lot of thought should be put into the actual writing. And two (or three or four) heads are better than one. So consider forming a committee for such a task and doling out portions of the plan to those with the most experience. The more ideas and suggestions contributed ensure the plan covers all areas of the operations and achieves goals set out in the beginning.

I recommend breaking the sections up and assigning the writing to those who may have some background in marketing, finance, or retail management. Then, after each person has written their section, have a meeting for everyone to share their ideas for the plan. Keep adding ideas as the plan progresses. Make it a group project, but make certain you give clear instructions on which section of the plan each will write and the timeframe / timeline required to get the project finished.

THINGS CHANGE

They say that the only sure things in life are 'death and taxes', but in actuality the only sure thing in life is **change**. The circumstances that were the basis of the first plan are constantly changing, so it will be necessary for you to review the original plan at least on an annual basis. More specifically, if the business plan is going to be effective to both the manager and volunteers, it needs to be revised as the circumstances change. That means any number of changes may occur in the operations of the gift shop throughout the year and any number of revisions made to the plan.

For example, the institution or facility where the shop is located may need to expand affecting your operations in terms of size and number of persons needed to man the shop.

Technology is constantly changing and any good business should keep up with these advances. Remember that the computer has replaced yesterday's typewriter and that email has replaced the antiquated airmail letter. You may need to upgrade computer equipment as needed or update credit card processing equipment. A good business plan will anticipate this need for change.

There will be constant changes in merchandise to purchase as customers' taste change. (Remember the beanie baby craze?) If your plan doesn't compensate for such fads, you'll find yourself with too many of something on hand or not moving fast enough to take advantage of the various trends.

You will need to constantly make changes to offer better customer service and more products that cater to the customer. Changes may also be required in your security plan as your shop expands and customer traffic increases.

All of this needs to be in the business plan and modified as needed. With every significant change in business, regardless of whether it is the merchandise or shoplifting prevention techniques, those changes need to be added (or deleted) in the plan.

With this in mind you will need to look at the original plan and modify it in order to reflect the changes. Review of the business plan. Schedule time to review your goals, compare your progress and revise the plan.

Understandably, this is an overwhelming task for one person so, again, put your volunteers to good use. Your volunteers have a wealth of knowledge. The volunteers working in the shop are in constant contact with the customers and would be your best source in assisting in updating the customer service sections of the plan. Your volunteer merchandise buyers can analyze buying trends, evaluate product sales, and identify new products coming to market, keeping the merchandise up to date. This buyer information is invaluable in modifying the plan.

Each organization is different and has different time constraints. So you'll need to determine what revisions and in what time frame are needed to change your plan, in order for the goals established to be accomplished.

Here's a quick example of a timeline for revised business planning that's worked for me:

Beg. of January   **Write the business plan outline**
                             Assign sections to various volunteers

End of January   **All assignments are due**

Beg. of February   **Board reviews plan**

Beg. of June   **Review goals, compare to current sales**
                             Adjust any marketing or sales goals
                             Updates regarding products due from buyers

Beg. of August   **Review goals, compare to current sales**
                             Prepare for holiday buying season

Chapter 3
Third Step: The Budget

Every business needs a budget. It's part of the plan! The budget is the single most important part of your business plan and is an integral part in helping your business achieving the goals you set for it.

But what exactly do you need to budget for? You may need to budget for the cost of building or remodeling if your shop requires such expenditures. If you are purchasing equipment, fixtures, display and supplies for the gift shop, you will need a budget for these expenditures. You **will** need a budget for the projection of sales, purchases, expense and profit for each calendar or fiscal year the business is in operation. A budget should be developed before you spend a cent, before you hire a contractor or make a purchase. Why? Well, among other reasons....so you won't overspend.

A budget is the guideline of the projects and purchases your business will create and make. A budget will help you realize what's important and what's not, what can be scheduled for later and what needs to be done now. It also gives you and your volunteers and workers a point of reference from which to work. Remember that saying..."Those who fail to plan, plan to fail," and nothing could be truer than those who fail to plan a budget. So let's get started making those budgets.

Here's a detailed look at each of the various types of budget you may need to formulate, who should serve on the committees to create each type of budget and what should be accomplished.

BUILDING OR REMODELING BUDGET:

For many new gift shops, the first budget you'll be working with is the building or remodeling budget. When starting out on a large project such as building or remodeling, you need to budget your funds for optimum results. Because there will be unexpected problems or issues that may crop up, armed with a budget you'll be able to easily overcome such problems and compensate for unexpected expenditures. Especially with any type of building or remodeling assume there will be unexpected expenditures!

Most likely the institution or facility will decide on a set amount for building and remodeling and they will make all the project decisions. Hopefully they will include the volunteers in the construction or remodeling of the space set aside for a gift shop.

 If this is the case, form a building or remodeling committee. Seek out persons to serve on the committee that have had some experience in building or remodeling. You will need persons with knowledge about electrical and plumbing installation. You will need persons with financial expertise. Check to see if those volunteering or those persons associated with your organization have experience in any of these fields. You may have a retired builder, architect, electrician, and plumber, purchasing agent or accountant in the group. Recruit them to share their knowledge in the development of the budget and the execution of the project.

In addition, you should have the treasurer of your organization or auxiliary, the shop manager and a representative from the institution or facility where the shop will be located, serve on the committee. Your treasurer will help with the financial aspects of the building/remodeling budget. The manager of the shop will be able to tell you the needs of the shop in size and fixtures. The institution or facility representative will establish the guidelines and restrictions required. This committee should research construction costs and cost of fixtures to be installed, solicit comparative bids, evaluate and select contractors.

Visit gift shops in your area. Get recommendations. Most volunteer operated shops are willing to share information about remodels, contractors, fixture suppliers as well as problems they may have encountered. In the beginning, seeing how others have done it will help you formulate what is necessary to accomplish your building or remodeling.

To come up with a complete picture of what's needed, the committee will research the needs of the shop, the required floor space and fixtures and machines needed for operations. Detail those items that need to be built, custom-made, purchased or changed. Be sure to include in the budget, items necessary for the convenience of the customer and the volunteer manning the shop such as wheelchair ramps, storage and convenient check-out counter. Once you've been able to identify the needs of both customer and volunteer/employee, have your committee review these improvements and start shopping for bids, to compare with the monies you have budgeted.

Chapter 6, "Successful Shop Set-Up" takes you through the steps necessary for building or remodeling. It includes a proposal letter to get things started. If there is not an existing shop or you need to remodel, this is the time to start. You have the budget!

ANNUAL SALES BUDGET:

The annual sales budget for a gift shop (or for that matter any other money making project) is intended to set goals on sales and profits. With these goals, everyone will have an idea of how much the shop plans to spend on the different items purchased for the gift shop. Where do you get these figures? Unlike a building or remodeling budget that has fixed costs, an annual sales budget can be more challenging to estimate.

The first place to start could be the previous years' sales. If this is your first year in business it will take a bit more work. You will need to take into consideration the size and type of gift shop, and then go out on a fact-finding mission, talking to the managers of other similar shops to get an idea of expected sales. They are your best source of information, and the more sales data you can get from them, the more accurate your projections will be. But make sure you choose the shops similar to your own. Gift shops run the gamut of different sales and business models, so be very cautious, then combine results into averages. Pay special attention to the mark-up (the amount each shop adds to the cost to arrive at a selling price). This will give you a good idea of what the market will bring, what the merchandise is selling for in your area.

Remember, what you are striving for is an accurate, but realistic picture of what you can expect for sales. Your budget will give the shop something to strive for, so set your goals and aim high, but do so conservatively with a dash of faith. So, even if you don't reach your projected sales, it will not be the end of the world, just the beginning. These projections should be used as a tool and a guideline.

The Budget On Paper

The first step for your budget should be allocating how the money is to be spent for the various purchases needed to stock the shelves. By now you have an idea of what the mark-up will be on the merchandise for sale, so armed with this and your list of purchases, this will give you an idea of how much profit the shop will realize.

Start your budgeting process with a preliminary meeting. Discuss strategy and priorities, realistic amounts, and the planning process. Prepare and distribute a simple budget form template. (A Budget Form ready to fill out is included in Chapter14, Business Forms) This will help familiarize each person with the format of a budget.

The committee should include the treasurer of your volunteer organization, the Manager of the shop, the accounting manager of the shop and the buyers. It would also be a good idea to ask around and see if in your volunteer organization there is a retired accountant. Invite this accountant to attend the annual meeting. Professional (volunteer) input will be invaluable as most can offer an objective viewpoint. Their expertise, too, will be an asset as your accounting and budgetary needs get more complex.

To help, I've included an example of a hospital gift shop budget that shows how to allocate for various expenditures. While your shop's projection will not be the same, you can see just what a budget should contain. Notice how sales slowly turn into profits over a period of time. This is a realistic way to approach a budget. This type of budget, too, will show each buyer just how much he or she can spend on merchandise they are tasked with purchasing.

Be aware however that some shops may pay out more in operating expenses; this example assumes that the shop is within the organization where most of the overhead is assumed by the administration or organization where you are volunteering. So be sure if your organization doesn't operate in a similar fashion to include the additional supply cost and expenses.

In the following budget example, the only supply costs are the supplies for the daily operation of the shop, like office supplies and customer service supplies and the only shop expenses is for the phone service. Yours may include many more. Aside from the following real life example, I've also included a blank budget for you to enter your own projections in *Appendix A - Business Forms*. Just copy the budget form. Make enough copies for each person in the budget committee meeting and get going on creating your plan for future sales success.

Remember, most printed and online examples and information about sales budgets are typically written for the regular retail business. Normally these forms and example budgets include items such as income tax, rent, loan payments, and overhead expenses. You typically will not have to deal with these items. The example in *Appendix A – Business Forms* is specifically for volunteer operated non-profit gift shops and list only items pertinent to this type of shop.

Budget for year ____ 200X____

	JAN	FEB	MAR	APR	MAY	JUN	JUL	AUG	SEP	OCT	NOV	DEC	TOTAL
Sales *(projected)*	7000	9000	9000	9000	8000	7000	7000	7000	8000	9000	10000	10000	100000
Sales tax	490	630	630	630	560	490	490	490	560	630	700	700	7000
Purchases:													
Candy	400	400	400	400	400	300	250	300	300	500	500	500	4650
Cards/paper	150	100	100	100	100	100	100	100	100	150	150	150	1400
Sundries	200	200	100	100	100	100	100	100	100	200	200	200	1700
Gifts	1000	500	500	500	750	750	500	500	750	750	1000	1000	8500
Flowers	700	1500	900	1000	1000	900	900	900	900	1000	1000	1000	12000
Plush/Toys	900	1000	1000	1000	800	900	1000	1000	1200	1800	1500	1500	13600
Jewelry	1000	750	500	500	200	200	500	500	500	1000	1500	1000	8150
Total Purchases													50000
Supplies:	50	25	25	25	25	25	25	25	25	50	50	50	400
Expenses:	100	75	75	75	75	75	75	75	75	100	100	100	1000

Notice how the purchase of some items increase in the months prior to a holiday. You will need to anticipate the increase in sales for different times of the year and budget the purchasing of merchandise accordingly.

The above budget is based on the assumption that the shop is already in operations and that you have existing merchandise to sell in the shop. If you were starting from scratch the purchases would, of course, be much larger in the months prior to setting up shop.

You can see by looking at this sample budget, listed on the previous page, that projected sales are based on the amount of goods you intend to purchase or have in the shop for sale.

Your expenses should be budgeted so you will have some idea of profit. Another expense included in finding profit is the cost of the merchandise that has been sold. An even though this cost is not projected in the budget. It will come into play when determining profit.

Next you'll learn how to determine exactly how to compute the profits for your shop.

Determining Profits

But where does profit come in to play? Profit (on paper) is actually derived from a standard business formula. This is a business formula used in accounting to determine the cost of the merchandise sold in a business that will determine the profit. This cost formula is an essential part of the budget and if you aren't familiar with this, pay special attention because profit isn't just what's left over. It's a little bit more complicated, so let me break it down in basic terms.

The cost of the merchandise sold is referred to as "cost of goods sold" (COGS). This formula is necessary for determining, not only the total amount of money you paid for the items sold in the shop, but also is necessary to arrive at the profit that the shop makes. This formula will show you are attaining your goals. If you have a positive number at the end, you're making profit. Negative numbers mean no profit. It's that simple.

BEGINNING INVENTORY	**$20,000**
+ PURCHASES	50,000
- ENDING INVENTORY	40,000
(physically taken in shop at end of first year)	

= COGS (cost of merchandise sold)	**$30,000**

SALES	**$100,000**
- SALES TAX (if applicable)	7,000
- EXPENSES & SUPPLIES	1,400
- COGS	30,000

= PROFIT	**$61,600**

In above example, it's assumed that the shop's BEGINNING INVENTORY value is $20,000. On the next line, you'll note that I've added in PURCHASES and that amount is $50,000. The assumption is that throughout the year, $50,000 worth of merchandise, at wholesale cost, is purchased for the shop to resell. It doesn't really matter when the merchandise is purchased. For example, maybe $10,000 is purchased at the first of the year and the rest at different times during the year. But what is important, is that the amount is tallied and included in the calculations.

Now, when an inventory is taken at the end of the year it is revealed that $40,000 worth of merchandise, at **WHOLESALE COST** is still remaining in the shop, unsold. This will happen. Don't expect everything you purchase to sell out. If it does, great! But if not, that's typical of any business. That's why taking inventories either at the end of the year or periodically will help you determine how sales are going.

The **cost** value of the remaining inventory was subtracted from the **cost** value of the merchandise purchased to give the wholesale **cost** of the merchandise sold during the year. (Retail value of the merchandise does not enter into the calculation for the "cost of goods sold".) Again, you paid wholesale, and you must determine the wholesale value of any inventory remaining to get an accurate picture of total profit.

Now to find out the **PROFIT!** The wholesale cost of merchandise that has been sold Cost of Goods Sold **COGS** and the other cost of doing business in the year (these other costs are taxes, business supplies and operating expenses) are subtracted from the amount of the **retail sales**. The remaining figure gives you the profit for a year or period. In this example, we did pretty well, and made a profit.

Even though I go into the explanation of business formulas in Chapter 13, I thought that an explanation of the COGS is important to understand when compiling the budget. Profit will always be on your mind.

I can't stress enough, the importance of establishing a budget for the gift shop operations. If you think about it, a budget is nothing more than a plan in numbers. A plan that helps you realize a profit and assure that the goals of the gift shop will be met.
Each year these goals will change and the numbers will change on the budget. Needless to say the projected numbers should go up!

As you develop a budget, think of it as the part of your plan you can most easily control. Consider your plan objectives, your sales and marketing activities, and how you'll relate your spending to your strategy and goals. Remember as you budget, you want to prioritize your spending to match your priorities in sales and marketing. The emphasis in your strategy should show up in your actual detailed programs. That's your budget!

Chapter 4

Fourth Step: The Paper Work

Making a budget and following your financial plan is just one step to success. The next step is keeping the paperwork in order. Your volunteer shop should be run like any other retail business. There is a misconception that it is not necessary to keep good records, apply for licenses or fill out tax forms since it's a non-profit or a small shop. Nothing could be further from the truth. Every shop within a non-profit organization or any shop that will be operated by volunteers cannot succeed unless it is run like a normal business and follows all the rules and regulations of business. You need to file tax forms, track money spent, apply for licenses, work with volunteers as you would employees, etc. so you will need to keep impeccable records.

If it is a requirement in the state where the shop is located, you may need to apply for a business license or tax identification number, just like any retail shop in your local shopping center would do. In states that have sales tax, the tax collected on sales must be reported and paid quarterly.

Yes, you must pay local taxes (if applicable), and each state, city and county has different tax requirements, so make sure you check. Some non-profits are not tax exempt. And tax requirements don't stop with the local tax man. Even though profits from the shop go to the organization as a donation and you do not pay federal income tax, you may need to report the income to the Federal Government. If your actual annual sales exceed a certain amount you will be required to file an **informational tax return** with the U. S. Internal Revenue Service at the end of the calendar or fiscal year.

According to the Federal tax laws, a business may choose an annual accounting period for keeping records and reporting income called a "tax year". The tax years can be based on the calendar year or a fiscal year. The calendar year is where you report your income and expenses from January 1 through December 31 of each year. A fiscal year is 12 consecutive months ending on the last day of any month except December. If you adopt a fiscal year basis you must report income and expenses on the same consecutive months each year. For more information refer to IRS Publication 538, "Accounting Period and Methods"

Although your volunteer organization will not actually pay an income tax, you may still need to file a return. This return verifies your tax-exempt status. If you do not maintain records and file correct data and proper paperwork, the IRS can (and has) declined tax-exempt statuses.

So, you can see how important it is to keep impeccable records. You should check with your state's requirements, as well as any changes to the federal tax laws. Remember state requirements are different, but the Federal Requirements are the same. In this chapter I will give you general instructions on how to apply for and comply with requirements to start up the shop.

FEDERAL REQUIREMENTS

Step #1
Applying for a FEDERAL EXEMPTION

Most likely the organization that the gift shop is a part of has already established a tax-exempt status with the U. S. Internal Revenue Department and applied for a Taxpayer's Identification Number. But if you are just establishing your volunteer organization and the gift shop, you will need to request **Publication 557**, a tax-exempt status for your organization, from the IRS. Filling out the information it asks for on the form is relatively easy to do and the IRS does include instructions with the form. Once you've filled it out, return the form to the address specified. Filing this application will provide your organization with a tax-exempt status under code 501(c). Make sure you make copies! Keep the copies filed with your other important papers, in a safe location.

Generally, tax-exempt organizations must file an annual information return with the IRS. Tax-exempt organizations that have annual gross receipts less than $25,000 are not required to file the annual informational return. Gross receipts (annual sales) over $25,000 must file a return. So you can see why keeping records is so important!

Tax-exempt organizations, other than private foundations, must file Form 990, Return of Organization Exempt From Income Tax, or Form 990-EZ, Short Form Return of Organization Exempt From Income Tax. The Form 990-EZ is designed for use by small tax-exempt organizations and nonexempt charitable trusts. An organization may file Form 990-EZ, instead of Form 990, only if (1) its gross receipts during the year were less than $100,000, and (2) its total assets (line 25, Column B of Form 990-EZ) at the end of the year were less than $250,000. If your organization's gross receipts were more than $100,000 and assets exceeded $250,000, file Form 990.

Form 990 or Form 990-EZ must be filed by the 15th day of the 5th month after the end of your organization's accounting period (calendar or fiscal year). The instructions for these forms indicate the Federal Service Center to which they must be sent. A tax-exempt organization that fails to file a required return is subject to a penalty of $20 a day for each day the failure continues. The same penalty will apply if the organization fails to give correct and complete information or required information on the return. Don't waste the hard-earned money you've made by failing to file on time. Keep a reminder on your calendar of when the various forms should be filed. It's best to send all forms via certified mail to show proof of when the form was mailed. Without such proof the IRS could penalize you if they do not receive the forms on time.

The forms filed on behalf of your volunteer organization should include a record of membership and services. That is, the total hours served by the membership of the organization, and the **cost equivalent figure** must be attached to the form to provide proof of the non-profit status. The cost equivalent is derived from the average per hour wage of hospital employees. The average per hour wage of a hospital employee is a figure set by and can be obtained from the Department of Health. This is used to equate the total amount of volunteer hours into a dollar amount. Are you starting to see how important it is to track everything? From sales to volunteer hours worked!

> *REMEMBER: These are just guidelines. Tax laws may have changed. Forms and procedures may have been modified since this book was printed. Check with the tax department.*

Step #2
Applying for a LOCAL STATE SALES TAX EXEMPTION

Currently, Alaska, Delaware, Montana, New Hampshire and Oregon do not have a state sales tax. So if the shop will be in one of those states you will not have to be concerned with this section but if the gift shop is in any of the other states, you will need to apply for a STATE SALES TAX EXEMPTION. (Remember to check however, as at the time of this printing, states such as Alaska were considering implementing a variety of different state sales taxes.)

You will need to apply for a tax exempt, resale permit or resale number from the state in which the shop will do business. You will apply to the comptroller's office of your state. Once received, this tax-exempt status will allow your gift shop to make tax-exempt purchases on products that you can then sell in the shop. It also means you will have to collect sales tax on sales to customers, and then remit all the state sales tax collected, during the year to the state.

When applying for the exempt status, the organization must write to the comptrollers' office of their state. Include, in your correspondence, a detailed description of the activities conducted by the organization, a copy of the organizations by-laws or articles of incorporation. If the organization is a corporation, send a list of all services performed by the organization. A copy of the letter you received from the U.S. Internal Revenue Service granting tax-exempt status with the U. S. Internal Revenue Department must also be included.

You will then be classified as a charitable non-profit organization and given a state resale number (state tax-exempt number).
Some states now offer the ability to apply online.

You will use this number to make purchases for the shop for resale. No one in the organization should abuse this resale number by purchasing merchandise for their personal use. **This is very important**. Why? The organization will risk losing its tax-exempt status if the number is used in the wrong manner. This means the number should not be given freely to just anyone. A person using this number should be authorized to make purchases solely for the organization. This number should never be used for any item purchased for anyone's personal use, only for items purchased for resale! Many non-profits have lost their tax-exempt status due to such abuse.

The state will require you to collect a sales tax on all retail items sold in the gift shop. It is the retailer's responsibility to collect state sales tax or accept, in good faith, an exemption certificate to exempt the collection of the sales tax. (People who live in tax-exempt states oftentimes request tax exemption as do other non-profit organizations.) You should keep accurate records of all taxes collected to make filling out the forms easier.

> **REMEMBER:** *Your state may have additional requirements for licensing and tax-exemptions.*

Once you've registered with the state, the state will send a form that outlines the tax that needs to be calculated and collected from the gift shop and when those forms are due. Typically the collection of the sales tax is done on a quarterly basis. And usually, most states forms are brief and relatively easy to understand. If you need help in filling out the forms, and are unsure, contact the state's comptroller's office or consult your accountant.

Most likely your state will require you enter your total sales for the period, which is typically quarterly, and the calculation used to collect the tax. You should make a copy of the form, then **remit payment** of tax promptly, noting the date and method of payment (check number, etc)

In most states, you may also need to file for a business license and you may be required to fill out city tax forms. You should check with the State Licensing Division of your state, and contact your city or county's tax collection department to see if the shop will need a business license or tax permit to conduct business.

Step #3
OTHER LICENSES

There may be other licenses or ordinances you may need to follow. For example, if live plants are sold in the shop you may need to get a license from the Agriculture Department.

And remember, if you are selling food products, check with your County Health Department for the local requirements. Even selling small amounts of produce may have specific requirements, and if you are preparing any food on site, you may have to get a license and rating from the local Health Department. Remember that many city Health Departments also do not allow for foods to be sold that were baked in private homes.

CHOOSING A BANK

Undoubtedly, you will need to set up a business account at a local bank. And these days it pays to shop around for a bank, since many now, have started charging a myriad of fees.

Get the business account information from, at least 3 banks, preferably the largest bank and two of the smaller banks in your area. Then you can compare fees and rates on the different types of accounts offered by each bank. Larger banks may have more options, but smaller banks may offer lower fees and friendlier customer service. The easiest way to gather this information is to call and request a brochure for business accounts or go to each bank's web site. The brochures and web sites will list the different types of business accounts offered by the bank, their rates and fees and rules and regulations. Some of the larger banks have information just for non-profit organization. Study the information to determine which bank and type of account is right for your shop.

Now, pay a visit to each bank, and interview the managers or small business representatives to find out what particular benefits the bank can offer a non-profit volunteer managed business.

You and the treasurer of your organization can compare fees and rates on the different types of account offered by each bank. Although you may be shooting for the lowest fees, keep in mind that volunteers may be doing the banking and a convenient location should be a part of your decision, especially if your gift shop handles large sums of money, and closes shop after the banking hours.

Unfortunately, free accounts extended to non-profits or volunteer organizations are a thing of the past, so you need to do some comparisons! But don't give up. Sometimes the personal interview of the bank's managers will lead to reduced fees.

Questions To Ask Every Bank

(Or as I like to call it, "Checking on Checking")

✓ **Do you have "interest bearing" business checking accounts?**
Some banks pay money market rates with a minimum balance, although the balance requirements may be high. Check out all the restrictions and chose the interest bearing account most suited to the business of the shop. You will be making frequent deposits and paying a number of bills each month and some accounts have a fee for each transaction or limit the number of free transactions. So you would not want to choose an account that charges or is limited to only a few free transactions a month. Also check into whether electronic transactions are included in the number of transactions. Some banks don't charge anything to have deposits or payments taken out of your account electronically; others charge more than normal "paper" transactions.

✓ **What are the minimum balances? What are the penalties?**
Penalties and additional banking fees can cut into your profits. Be sure you find out exactly and understand what is required for the type of account you are considering and the penalties imposed.

✓ **What about freebies like printed checks, and endorsement stamps?**
Many banks now charge upwards of $30 or more for printed checks. And if you have to purchase an endorsement stamp, factor that all into your side-by-side analysis of each bank. Hidden costs can actually make doing business with a relatively inexpensive bank more costly.

✓ *Is there a fee for making deposits over $1000?*

Believe it or not, banks are now charging you for depositing money! Yes, believe me, some banks charge a fee for making deposits over $1,000 into a business account and may put lengthy holds on large deposit sums, preventing you from using that money.

✓ *Does the bank return your canceled checks?*

This can be an important factor in choosing a bank because balancing your check book or checking files is easier when you have copies of the checks. Some banks will charge you to do research to find a check if you need to verify that check.

✓ *Are there options for acceptance of credit cards and check verification?*

Most large banks will have a package for the small business that includes all these financial aspects. Some may charge additional fees for processing each item. Others may charge you a reconciliation fee, so double-check.

✓ *Do they offer online banking?*

Most banks now are offing on-line banking. You don't have to wait until the end of the month to get a balance, see if a check has cleared, or get a copy of a cancelled check. This can all be done on line. Most banks offer this as a free service. **Check** this out!

Opening a Business Checking Account

Once you've decided on which bank gives you the best value for your money and you are ready to open an account, you will need to take along the following documents required to open a business account:

1. **By-laws of the organizations** or if you are incorporated a copy of the Certificate of Incorporation

2. **A list of the officers** of the organization

3. **The federal tax ID number**
   (not to be confused with your tax exempt number)

4. **A copy of your business license**
   (not every state requires this for non-profits but if yours does bring it)

5. **Photo identification**

Remember the bank requires that the signature of each person signing on the account be on file. So, if the president, treasurer and gift shop manager will all be writing checks on the account, you may want to set a convenient time to visit the bank together. This way opening the account can be accomplished in only one trip. Remind everyone to take along their photo ID. This is also a great way for them to get acquainted with the bank where they will be making deposits and transacting other banking business. Another suggestion - make an appointment to open the account with the bank manager, in advance.

Finally, it is a good idea to establish a merchant status with the bank to set up your credit card transactions. Typical fees for processing credit card transactions and crediting the amount of the purchases charged to your account range from 1.5 to 6.05% of each sale, in addition to transaction fees (typically from .05 to .45 cents per transaction), plus monthly reporting fees and fees for the use of the credit card processing terminal. The higher the volume of credit card sales the lower the percentage of each sale.

After you have established an account at a bank, cultivate a relationship with the manager and always present yourself in a professional manner. If a problem arises, knowing the manager can't hurt.

Chapter 5
Fifth Step: The Gift Shop Manual

Any business needs a guide to run smoothly. That guide is called a 'Manual of Operations". In some situations, where the shop is not complex and is relatively small, the operations manual could take the place of a business plan. Both, a business plan and/or operations manual will outline how the business will operate, establish policies and procedures and outline information about merchandising, markets, suppliers and customers.

Now that you have the basic business necessities of 'setting up shop' out of the way, the next step is to outline your day-to-day business operations and compile a manual of operations.

The manual will provide a foundation and structure for the shop. It will provide a day by day guide to operating all phases of the shop. It will establish the policies and procedure used in the shop.

The persons working in the shop will know exactly what is expected of them. It will help them understand their roles and responsibilities. Any business owner or manager who runs a successful business knows the importance of written procedures. Written procedures provide guidelines to ensure that everything that needs to be done, gets done.

With well-defined policies and procedures you eliminate the need to make decisions over and over again about what should be done. You outline what daily steps are needed to make sure the gift shop runs smoothly. Keep in mind, that as the shop grows or as needs arise, policies and procedures will need to be reviewed and revised, just as in the business plan and budget.

The established policies provide the shop attendant with an answer to all questions that arise in the course of business and the established procedures with an answer to all the questions on operations within the shop.

To get started in writing policies and procedures for your shop, think about each problem that could occur and about each task that needs to be done during the business day. Next, write down step-by-step instructions to solve the each problem or accomplish each task. Write them in such a manner, as if you were actually there talking to a person and guiding them through each step. Make sure you first explain what needs to be done, then create a list of steps to solve the problem or accomplish the task.

Trying to think of EVERYTHING that needs to be done, and every circumstance that may arise may seem overwhelming. So, enlist the help of the volunteers to help you write clear instructions for each task in the shop since they are the ones who are closest to the source. And if your shop is just starting out, or the amount of volunteers for this project are limited, have the person in your organization that has had experience with office machines write down a step-by-step guide on the operation of the cash register. Have the 'diplomat' in your group detail ways to handle customer complaints. Perhaps you have someone in your organization that has flair with design. Have them write a step-by-step section on how to create engaging and eye-catching displays.
Then edit and compile them into a manual or instructions for operations.

When you develop written policies and procedures you give the shop the consistency and stability the volunteer and customer deserve. Just think about trying to run a computer without a manual. The beasts are not very intuitive, are they? Neither is operating a gift shop, especially for those volunteers and workers who may never have worked in retail before. Periodically, hold volunteer meetings where you review a section of the manual, soliciting feedback on ways it can be improved.

Use the following sample manual as a framework or outline to get you started on your own. Or you can just fill in the blanks to personalize and copy for your shop's use.

A copy of the completed manual should be given to each volunteer, during the gift shop orientation. There should be a manual for reference in the gift shop at all times.

The best method I've found for binding such a manual is to use a three-ring binder, with tab dividers for easy access to each section. That way you can add new sections, remove outdated sections and easily update any page. Plus 3-ring binders make the manual more "user friendly" and give volunteers the ability to jot down notes about procedures that may need updating or revising.

If you want to start your own manual from scratch, here are section titles I'd recommend including:

- ✓ **DAILY POLICIES AND PROCEDURES**
- ✓ **DAY AND EVENING SHIFT PROCEDURES**
- ✓ **CASH REGISTER OPERATIONS**
- ✓ **CREDIT CARDS INSTRUCTIONS**
- ✓ **CUSTOMER SERVICE**
- ✓ **POSITIONS & THEIR DUTIES**

And this is an important final point to emphasize when writing a manual. This manual will be used while the shop is open, so getting to the point is very important. Volunteers and workers may not have the time to leisurely read over the manual when a customer is standing right there waiting to buy a product. You need to give your workers concise information in an easy to read, quickly accessible format.

GIFT SHOP MANUAL

(EXAMPLE)

BUSINESS CONCEPTS

The GIFT SHOP of _____ is run by the MEMBERS
of the _____. Success of the Gift Shop depends on the
support of ALL MEMBERS.

The Gift Shop operations will be professionally carried out in accordance
with the BY- LAWS of _____, the POLICIES set forth in
this manual and the approval of the ADMINISTRATION of

_____.

The goal of the Gift Shop is to raise money for the Organization. The
profits of the shop shall be used to benefit the objectives of the
Organization.

The Gift Shop Volunteers will strive for increase in profits, remaining
flexible in MARKET OBJECTIVES, adjusting these objectives, as needs
dictate with the growth of the Organization.

POLICIES & PROCEDURES

DRESS CODE: Established by the POLICIES of ORGANIZATION (Description of dress code, uniforms, etc)

SHOP HOURS: ___: ___ a.m. till ___: ___ p.m.

SHIFT: Clock in when reporting for your volunteer shift, record volunteer hours. If unable to work your regular shift, give advanced notice to Gift Shop SCHEDULING COORDINATOR. Find a substitute. (Substitute list will be posted in shop)

SECURITY LOCK ALL valuables in provided lockers.

SAFETY Do not wear expensive jewelry while on duty. Do not bring items of personal value, checkbook, credit cards or large amounts of cash to the shop, while on duty.

FOLLOW procedures set by organization's SECURITY. NEVER leave shop unattended, if attending the shop alone and you need to leave for a break **LOCK** the door and post a sign as to the **time you will return**. Inform the INFORMATION DESK or SWITCHBOARD.

SHOPLIFTING

THEFT: Make eye contact and greet each customer that enters the shop. Be attentive to all customers, assisting with selections. Call security if you observe shoplifter leaving with merchandise. Take note of the appearance of the suspected shoplifter and the item in question. **Do not approach the suspect.**

FIRE: **In immediate area:**
alert all persons in shop, lock shop,
if time; evacuate to outside of building, through nearest exit.

Not in the immediate area: alert all persons in shop; make sure all doors are closed with-in the shop. Lock shop and exit outside building and wait for all clear sign. Take keys with you.

DISASTER: Alert all persons in shop. Close and lock door. Report to information desk or listen for announced instructions.

REVIEW THE BUILDINGS SECURITY & SAFETY PROCEDURES!

DISCOUNTS: 10% to ALL VOLUNTEERS and EMPLOYEES
EXCEPTIONS: NO discounts on Candy, Gum, Flowers, Balloons, Gift Baskets, Drugs and Sundries, Greeting Cards, Paper Products and SALE ITEMS.

EXCHANGES: NO EXCHANGES on merchandise that has been taken into a sick room (pertaining to hospital shops). NO EXCHANGES on EDIBLES or FLOWERS. Encourage the customer to find like item to make exchange, as there are NO CREDITS OR REFUNDS.

REFUNDS: NO REFUNDS OR CREDITS.

CREDITS: EXCEPTION - **DEFECTIVE MERCHANDISE** a refund or credit will be made only on defective merchandise, within 7 days from date of purchase with receipt.

EXCEPTION - **REASONABLE** request for refunds or credit within the SAME DAY. (Can be treated as a void and the merchandise returned to stock.)

CHECKS: Accept checks on **in state** banks, **ONLY.**
Checks accepted for the **AMOUNT OF PURCHASE.**

GENERAL PUBLIC - NO counter checks!
Accept only PRINTED CHECKS with Name, Address and Phone # .
All information must be current.
Ask to SEE the customer's DRIVERS LICENSE.
Legibly, write the License # and expiration date on check
Check the PHOTO ID and **return** the license.
Use **check verification** (if applicable).

EMPLOYEE: Write their department and ext. # on check.
VOLUNTEER: Write "Volunteer" on check. Verify volunteer status. Do **NOT** accept **POSTDATED** checks.

CHARGE CARD: Visa, Master Card, Discover, American Express

Check hologram on for valid card.

Check picture ID.

CHECK THE EXPIRATION DATE.

Follow instructions under CHARGE CARDS.

SHOP CHARGE: (If applicable)

EMPLOYEE

PAYROLL DEDUCTIONS (EPD):

(If applicable)

A ledger card is maintained for each employee account or an EPD. Form is filled out for each purchase to be sent to the payroll department.

Only one employee payroll deduction purchase, at a time. Deduction to be taken from employee pay check starting on the next pay period. No less than 25% of total purchase.

Minimum purchase $25.00.

Employee Payroll Deduction can be paid in full at any time. Follow instructions under EMPLOYEE PAYROLL DEDUCTIONS.

LAYAWAYS:

(If applicable) A layaway record ticket is prepared for each layaway. Minimum lay-a-way $25.00.

One lay-a-way per customer, at a time.

No adding to lay-a-way or taking items, until lay-a-way is PAID IN FULL. 25% of total lay-a-way is required as down payment. The lay-a-way will be held for 3 months. If merchandise is not paid in full at the end of the 3 months, the merchandise in the lay-a-way will be returned to stock and deposit and payments forfeited by customer. Customer will be notified by mail 2 weeks before the 3 months has elapsed.

Follow instructions under LAY-A-WAY.

HOLDS: Merchandise will be put on HOLD for ___ days.
FILL OUT hold form, attach to merchandise and store in HOLD BIN.

APPROVAL: Merchandise will not be taken from shop on approval.

THE ABOVE POLICIES ON CHECKS, CHARGE, LAYAWAYS & HOLDS WILL BE POSTED IN THE SHOP

DAMAGED MERCHANDISE:

Remove from stock and put in storeroom. Attach a note identifying the damage From time to time merchandise will be accidentally damaged or broken. Usually this is the fault of the way it was displayed. Do not worry about this; it is a COST OF DOING BUSINESS. Assure customer if accident occurs, not to feel bad, but graciously accept reimbursement if offered.

PRICING: If you run across an item that is not priced, return it to the storeroom to be re-priced.
If customer picks up item without price sticker, look for a like item to quote price.
BE AWARE of PRICE SWITCHING!

STOCKING: If time permits, restock items.

DAILY OPERATIONS
SUGGESTIONS TO MAKE THE DAY GO SMOOTHER:

- ✓ Greet customer, with eye contact, as they enter the shop.

- ✓ DO NOT put money received from customer in CASH REGISTER until change is given.

- ✓ COUNT the change to the customer.

- ✓ Wrap the merchandise in tissue and sack along with the customer's receipt.

- ✓ Avoid turning back to customer.

- ✓ Do not leave shop unattended.

- ✓ Become especially attentive when groups of young people enter shop.

- ✓ Try to discourage children from loitering and handling merchandise.

- ✓ Carefully observe people carrying large handbags and shopping bags.

- ✓ Be attentive to customers carrying merchandise from one location to another.
  (Offer to hold the merchandise at the check-out counter)

- ✓ Do not allow merchandise to lie around a counter, if it belongs elsewhere.

START OF SHIFT PROCEDURE

✓ RECORD VOLUNTEER HOURS in VOLUNTEER ROOM /CLOCK

✓ UNLOCK shop and turn on lights.

✓ CHECK REGISTER and preparing shop for business.

✓ COUNT THE MONEY in the CASH DRAWER
  ($_____ in cash and coins).

✓ Arrange calculator, credit card sales slip, and other items needed
  for convenient access during your shift.

✓ CHECK BULLETIN BOARD for MESSAGES or NEW
  MERCHANDISE information.

✓ Walk through the shop and see that everything is neat and in order.

✓ Replenish stock as needed, especially fast moving items.
  (candy & gum)

✓ OPEN DOOR to shop and take out Lobby Displays.

YOU ARE READY FOR YOUR FIRST SALE!

For any **PROBLEM** with CASH REGISTER or CHARGE CARDS refer to the titled instructions.

IF YOU FIND AN ITEM WITHOUT A PRICE STICKER OR TAG, PLEASE PUT THE ITEM ON MARKING SHELF.

Feel free to "DUST & ADJUST" merchandise on shelves. Try to keep items near the same location. This way we can keep track of the merchandise. But use your creative abilities. It is YOUR SHOP, SO, HAVE FUN!!!

END OF THE SHIFT PROCEDURE

✓ Bring LOBBY DISPLAYS into shop.

✓ LOCK ALL DOORS TO SHOP.

✓ RUN CASH REGISTER PRINT-OUT FOR TOTALS

✓ Enter amounts on the RECONCILIATION REPORT. If not indicated on register print out journal tape, add checks, then credit cards, and subtract from sales total. This will give you the correct amount of cash. Enter on the report.

✓ SETTLE/BALANCE the Charge Card TRANSACTIONS.
THE TRANSACTIONS MUST BE SETTLED DAILY
DETAILED INSTRUCTIONS ARE IN THE CHARGE CARD SECTION.

✓ Put CASH, CHECKS, CHARGE CARD SALES SLIPS, SETTLEMENT SLIP in Sales Report envelopes provided, along with Daily & Reconciliation reports and cash register printout. PUT YOUR NAME & DATE on out-side of envelope.

✓ COUNT the CASH remaining in the drawer. Leaving _____ for the next shift. (If the drawer is over or under, adjust from the OVER/UNDER money Take out or put in, as the case maybe, to balance the cash at an even ____).

✓ CLOSE CASH DRAWER.

✓ Put ENVELOPE containing DAILY RECEIPTS and PETTY CASH BOX in safe and LOCK.

✓ Turn OFF lights.

✓ LOCK DOOR then CHECK DOOR - **RECHECK DOOR!**

Gift Shop Manager

Duties:

- Appoint an **Assistant**
- Appoint Scheduling Manager
- Appoint Accounting Manager
- Appoint **Departmental Buyers**
- Work with Volunteer Coordinator to staff shop
- Provide training of sales staff
- Post GIFT SHOP policies in shop
- Conduct Monthly Sales Meetings
- Submit BUDGET at annually for approval
- Coordinate BUYERS and oversee purchases
- Check all purchases orders, invoices and statements
- Submit all INVOICES (Initialed and dated) PROMPTLY for payment (Bills PAID ONLY from INVOICES)
- Responsible for daily sales receipts
- Determining a merchandise mark-up to assure a profit
- Check slow movers for mark-downs
- Check for reorders
- Provide PUBLICITY and ADVERTISING FOR SHOP
- Submit an ANNUAL REPORT to the Administration of Organization

The Gift Shop Manager, in service to the Organization shall strive to conduct the operation of the shop in a business like manner, **consider all suggestions and constructive criticism**, act as a liaison between each organization members, the Administration of the institution/facility and the community.

Assistant/CO-Manager

Duties:

- See to the Daily Operation
- Provide necessary forms and supplies for daily business
- See that all merchandise is priced
- Conduct all inventories

Accounting Manager

Duties:

- Bookkeeper for the shop
- Keep daily receipt records
- Make deposits
- Pay all bills
- Compile all financial reports

Scheduling Manager

Duties:

- See that the shop is staffed
- Post monthly calendar with work schedule
- Take part in staff training
- Compile and post current **Substitute List**

MERCHANDISING

BUYERS:

Departments: (Suggestions)

Candy & Gum - Drugs & Sundries

Gift Items

Greeting Cards - Paper Products

Jewelry

Plush/Toys

Duties:

- Coordinate buying with approval of Gift Shop Manager

- Keep current catalogs, for ordering, on file in Gift Shop

- Meet with Sales Representatives to place orders

- Take part in Workshops, Gift Shows, Buying Trips

- Attend Monthly Sales Meetings

- Unpack and check all incoming merchandise with packing slip

- Price and display in shop

- Attain, record and disperse all paper work

TIPS FOR BUYERS:

- ✓ Schedule meetings with Sales Reps. (Do NOT meet with Sales Reps in the Gift Shop. Use office or other private area.)
- ✓ When buying, keep in mind the PRICE the item will SELL for NOT COST. THINK RETAIL WHEN BUYING!
- ✓ Buy according to the customers needs and desires.
- ✓ Target the customers of the Gift Shop.
- ✓ Know your market! Do market research: Visit other Gift Shops, Card Shop, etc. to be aware of what is on the market.
- ✓ Review periodically what items are selling and what is not.
- ✓ Do not become overly enthusiastic about a new item without thinking through the practical side. It is a good idea to stay away from fads and trends. Taking advantage of a vendor's quantity discount may not be the wisest thing to do. (Purchase of large quantities may present a storage problem or the item may become obsolete.)
- ✓ Do not handle the same merchandise as the large discounters. It is virtually impossible to compete or undersell them.
- ✓ Learn how to say **NO** to salespeople. The salesperson may not have the shops best interest at heart and may be trying to unload merchandise that is not salable.
- ✓ Use the limited funds for purchases to stock what the customer wants. The needs and desires of the customer is the real key. Remember that for a customer to make a purchase, they must feel that they are receiving more from the purchase than the price of the purchase.
- ✓ **Remember that the market place is constantly changing!**

Organization Policy for Buyers and Buying Trips

The Organization will pay for ____buying trip(s) to the _____

_____Mart, each year, includes transportation and lodging. The buyer will

pay for food, drink and personal items.

Only to make the minimum order requirement can a personal purchase be
made at cost. These personal purchase selections made by buyers must
be handled through and paid for in the shop, so that state tax may be
collected. For merchandise other than cost, the merchandise is marked at
the gift shop's retail price and a discount (if applicable) is applied.

When making orders and reorders through catalog, vendors and sales
representatives, the buyer should not take advantage of the shop's tax ID
number or buy personal items using the organization's name.

As a buyer, I agree to the above guidelines:

_____

Signed & Dated

- Incoming shipments should be put BEHIND COUNTER OR IN SHOPROOM until processed. OPEN BOXES of merchandise should NEVER be left on showroom floor.

- Locate packing slip or invoice.

- Check number of items received against packing slip or invoice.

- Check condition of merchandise.

- Indicate any damage or discrepancy and notify MANAGER or BUYER.

- NOTIFY Vendor or Wholesaler IMMEDIATELY if any items are missing or damaged. Have ready, the invoice number, order number, date of order, item number, item description, cost, and loss or extent of damage, when making claim.

- Sign and date packing slip or invoice, Make **3 copies.**

- Original to MANAGERS FILE along with one copy, one for GIFT SHOP FILE and one for BUYER'S record.

- PRICE merchandise as suggested or by the shop's formulas.

PRICING

This guide for pricing will be competitive and assure that the shop will make a profit without gouging their customers. Mark-up of at least 100% on most items. DOUBLE THE COST. The term used in retailing when you double the cost is called is called "keystoning".

> *Remember: Always **INCLUDE** the shipping cost when determining mark-up!*

Formulas:

Gifts, Toys, Plush,

Apparel & Accessories:	**Cost x 2.1 + shipping**
Jewelry:	**Cost x 2.5**
Sundries:	**Cost x 1.5 to 2 or suggested retail**
Cards:	**Suggested retail**
Candy:	**Cost x 1.5 to 1.75 or suggested retail**
Specialty Candies:	**Cost x 1.75 to 2 or suggested retail**
Flowers:	**Negotiate with florist or Cost of materials & flowers x 2.5**

Occasionally items can be purchased at an exceptional discount and should be priced at suggested retail or what the market will bring.

REDUCTION of SELLING PRICE:

Items should be selectively purchased so there is little need for reduction of price. **REMEMBER THAT YOU LOSE MONEY ON ANY ITEM THAT IS REDUCED BY MORE THAN 50%.**

ADVERTISING

In-house:

- Elevator display cases
- Lobby posters
- Flyers
- Table Toppers in a Cafeteria or Lobby

Outside:

- Articles in community newspapers
- Internet web site
- Local Bulletin Board advertising

INVENTORY

- Maintain quality and quantity of merchandise through buyers
- Take a physical inventory annually at the end of the fiscal year or calendar year
- Inventory shall be valued at COST, as the retail price is a negotiable and a variable figure. The value of the merchandise for replacement is valued at COST

*IMPORTANT! The **RETAIL PRICE** of the merchandise should be included in the inventory list, only to provide a reference!*

DETERMINING COST OF GOODS SOLD:

Beginning Inventory at cost

+ Purchases

= Cost of Goods available for sale

- Ending Inventory at cost

= Cost of Goods Sold

NOTE: To arrive at the COST OF GOODS SOLD the RETAIL amount is irrelevant.

To find **PROFIT:**

Sales

- Cost of Goods Sold

= Profit

METHODS OF PAYMENT

CASH REGISTER OPERATION

Your cash register should come with an instruction manual. Condense the instructions for a step-by-step guide for the person operating the cash register. Include in this guide the illustrations found in the manual, labeling the different parts of the register, the illustrated instruction for replacing the cash register journal tape. The instructions for this cash register operation guide should contain the procedures 'to open the register for business', 'to record a sale', 'to correct mistakes' and 'to close the register at the end of the shift'. For example, the instructions for recording a sale should have an illustration or image of the register's keyboard with all keys labeled. Following is an example of a written procedure for a manual operated cash register.)

TO RECORD A SALE:

1. Assemble the item to be purchased on one side of the register.
2. Scan or manually enter each item into register.
3. As you enter or scan the item in the register, move them to the opposite side of the register or bag them.

For manual operated cash registers items 4 thru 8 only:

4. Enter the amount of purchase. (If the item is $5.98, press the 5 key, the 9 key and the 8 key)

5. Press the TAX key.

6. Press SUBTOTAL. (giving the amount of sale, including the tax)

7. Enter the method of payment from customer. CASH/TEND—CHECK—CHARGE. If cash and the customer will receive change, enter the AMOUNT of cash tendered, after you have pressed SUBTOTAL. The drawer will open and the register display will indicate the amount of change to be returned to the customer. (If the exact amount is tendered for the sale then press CASH TEND)
    Paying by check, press CHECK.
    Paying with charge card press CHARGE CARD.

8. If one than one item is purchased press the TAX key after entering the amount of EACH item.

9. Bag/sack/box merchandise and include receipt with purchase.
    Note: You should adapt these procedures in your Gift Shop Manual. Remember the instructions should be in detail and include all the basic steps. Write the instructions, assuming the person operating the cash register had never seen the machine before. If possible, copy and paste the illustrations into the manual right from the cash register's users manual or owners guide or use a digital camera to take pictures of the register and its screen within the various steps of a sale. Include in the instructions a section on 'what to do if things go wrong'.

CHARGE CARD INSTRUCTIONS

As with the cash register, the method of processing credits cards will vary from shop to shop. Your shop might lease or purchase a terminal or you may have a more sophisticated set up where the card is read through the register. You will be given instruction when you set up the credit card operations.

The instructions should include a step by step guide for each of these situations:

- When a credit card is presented for purchase in the shop
- When the magnetic strip on the customer's card is not readable/manual entry
- When a credit card is used for a phone order
- When a credit card sale needs to be voided
- How to balance or settle the credit card sales at the end of a shift
- When the credit card settlement is out of balance
- The 800# to call for assistance with credit card problems

The procedures will vary with the equipment you select in the shop.

(The following is a suggestion of how you might set up the credit card instruction in this manual. The first example will show you how to list the instructions for a credit card sale in the shop. The second example will address the phone order credit card sale. You should assume that the shop attendant making the credit card transaction has never done it before and has never viewed the equipment to be used.

CREDIT/DEBIT CARD INSTUCTIONS (In Shop)

1. Assemble merchandise to be purchased

2. Accept card from customer

3. Check card for valid hologram and expiration date

4. Enter the sale, as usual, in the register as charge card sale

5. Slide the card. (card reader on register or terminal)

6. Fill out a credit card sales receipt (if applicable)

7. Have customer SIGN the receipt

8. KEEP THE SHOP'S COPY

9. Give the customer their copy along with their CREDIT CARD

10. Sack merchandise

CREDIT CARD INSTRUCTIONS FOR PHONE ORDERS

(If you are manning the shop alone and have a customer, when a phone customer phones to place an order, take their name of the person calling and their phone number, explaining that you will return their call).

Follow these eleven steps for taking phone orders:

TO AVOID MISTAKES, ASK THE FOLLOWING QUESTIONS:

1. Type of card (Visa, Master Card, Discover, American Express)
    The shop attendant should state the credit card that the Gift Shop accepts at the beginning of the conversation

2. Name of person placing order

3. Their phone number

4. Their address

5. Their credit card number

6. The expiration date on the card

7. Description of merchandise to be ordered

8. The name and location of the person receiving the merchandise ordered.

9. Gift-wrap

10. Message on gift card

11. Manually enter the credit card number and record pertinent information on receipt/record of sale

12. Wait for approval of credit card sale

13. Does phone customer want transaction receipt mailed to them

POINT OF SALE SYSTEM (POS)

(Note: Training and instructions come with the system. Condense and include the instruction in the manual. As in the instructions for manual operated machines, you must provide a written step-by-step guideline. Starting from the time the system is tuned on until you log off at closing time.

This is a superior system for accepting payment. They help merchants process a wider variety of payment options--such as credit cards, smart cards, debit cards, electronic checks, check guarantee services and electronic benefit transfer cards offered by state and federal agencies. The POS eliminates the manual key-in processes.

Today's processing systems offer so many choices that merchants should seek the assistance of experts before making a final buying decision. The system will include a bar code scanner, magnetic stripe reader, cash drawer and receipt printer.)

LAY-A-WAY INSTRUCTIONS

Establishing: Lay-a-way minimum purchase $25.00 or more. (one or more items). The lay-a-way record/contract ticket should include:

Customers' name, complete address, home and work phone numbers, date, and total amount of items to be put in layaway, plus the sales tax.
Amount of down payment:
25% or more of total purchase.

Layaway transactions are entered into cash register in the following order:

Amount of each item, subtotal, tax, layaway key and down payment amount in the form of cash, check or charge. Give customer a duplicate receipt.
Leave price tags on merchandise and sack or box items. Remove the bottom of the layaway ticket and staple securely to packaged items. Put on storage shelf. File top portion of ticket in layaway file.

Payments: Lay-a-way payments are entered in cash register as layaway payment and amount of payment deducted from the lay-a-way ticket on file. Give customer receipt.

Final payment: When total amount is paid off mark "paid in full" on the ticket and give the merchandise to the customer checking with the customer that the merchandise is in good order

Lay-a-way can be paid in full at any time.

Lay-a-ways shall be paid off with-in 6 months.

The customer will be notified, by mail, 2 weeks before the 6 months holding period for lay-a-ways has elapsed. The customer must be told that if the merchandise is not paid off with-in the 6-month period, the merchandise will be returned to stock and the down payment and all monthly payments will be forfeited. No exceptions!

LAY-A-WAY PURCHASE CONTRACT

LAY-A-WAY #_32_____

Date: _____0-00-00_____

Shop Name: _____Museum Gift Shop_____

Address: _____000 Art Avenue_____

_____City_____

Phone: _____000-000-0000_____

Customer: _Miss Museum Patron_____

Address: _Patron Avenue_____

_City_____

Phone: _____000-000-0000_____

Description of Merchandise: **Price**

_____A Painting_____ $100.00___

_____A Sculpture_____   75.00___

Tax   12.69___

Total $187.69___

Less deposit (25%)   46.92___

Balance Due $140.77___

I agree to make weekly ___ monthly _X_ payments of $ __46.92__ , paying off the balance by ___4/0____ , _20__ . I understand that the merchandise will be returned to stock and that I will forfeit the money already paid, if merchandise is not claimed and paid for by this date.

Customer's Signature: _____Museum Patron_____

Payment Record

Date   Received by   Amount Paid Balance Due

_____

_____

_____

_____

NAME_____ LAY-A-WAY #_____

PHONE _____

PICK UP DATE_____

2-page form with label for merchandise.

Original - Shop Copy - Customer

EMPLOYEE PAYROLL DEDUCTIONS

- A ledger card will be maintained for each employee payroll deduction account to be sent to the payroll department, monthly for deductions from employees' paycheck.
- Fill out contract for Employee Payroll Deduction.
- Only one employee payroll deduction purchase, at a time.
- Amount of deduction to be taken from employee paycheck starting on the next pay period. No less than 25% of total purchase.
- Minimum purchase $25.00.
- Employee Payroll Deduction can be paid in full at any time.
- Employee Payroll Deductions are entered on cash register as purchase. Use the employee payroll deduction key for method of payment. This will enter the sales into the daily receipt, but not record any payment.
- When employee payroll deduction contract is paid in full, indicate on the ledger that it has been paid, so when the ledger cards go to the payroll department, the amount will not be deducted.

CONTRACT INCLUDES:

1. Customer's name, complete address, homes and work phone numbers, department with extension number and total amount of items purchased on the employee payroll deduction plan.
2. List purchases, describe each item. Total all the items and add tax. This is the **total of the purchase.**
3. Percentage of amount to be deducted each month.
4. The employee signature indicating that the merchandise is in their possession.
5. Have the employee read the contract before signing.

The contract has three copies. The top copy is attached to a ledger sheet that will be sent to the payroll department of the organization, the middle copy that is filed in the gift shop and the bottom copy to be given to the employee.

Example Contract for Employee Payroll Deduction Purchase:

EMPLOYEE PAYROLL DEDUCTION CONTRACT

Date: _____0/0/2000_____
Employee Name: _____Bookkeeping_____
Extension #: _____0000_____
Home Address: __000 Street_____
__Any Town_____
Home Phone ____000-000-0000_____

Merchandise
Purchased: _____Any Item_____$5.00
_____Another Item_____6.99
_____Another Item_____18.50

Amount of Purchase: $ __$30.49___
Tax: 2.21
Total: $32.70

Amount to be deducted monthly: $ _____$8.18_____ 25% of total

I authorize _____The Name of the Gift Shop_____ to deduct the above amount from my payroll check each pay period, starting on ___0/0/00___until the above total amount is paid in full. I further authorize ____The Gift Shop__, in the event of my termination, to apply my final payroll check towards my indebtedness, in accordance with Federal regulations. I agree to pay any remaining balance.

I have possession of the above merchandise.

_____*Employee Purchaser*_____
Employee's Signature

_____*Volunteer Attendant*_____
Shop Attendant's Signature

Coded on _____ by_____

3-page form:
Original-Accounting
1st Copy - Shop
2nd Copy– Employee

GIFT SHOP INTERNAL DIRECTORY

In your manual you should include its own personal "yellow pages" of sorts, which includes all phone and fax numbers, websites and e-mail addresses that might be used in the course of business for your employees. You might even include the list of members in the organization, along with their email addresses. Some of the important contact information to include:

- Security
- Organization
- President of Organization
- Treasurer of Organization
- Administration of the Institution or Facility
- Building Maintenance
- Bank
- Credit Card Help
- Credit Card Supplies
- Florist
- Refrigerated Cases
- Phone Company
- Suppliers 800 Numbers

(END OF MANUAL)

CHAPTER 6
Sixth Step: Setting Up the Store

The business plan is written, state and federal tax applications have been filed, budgets have been made, the manual is completed, and thoughts and ideas of a new shop are floating in the air. Hopefully you fast forwarded to this chapter back when you were making budgets and the construction or remodeling is already in progress. But if not, now is the time!

The involvement of your volunteer organization in the planning and construction of a new shop will vary with the administration of the non-profit or not-for-profit organization you represent. An existing shop may be up and running or a new shop or expansion is in the planning stages. Regardless, the volunteer organization is often asked for their input. Even if you aren't asked - offer it! Be prepared with lots of suggestions to get that near perfect shop, because it will be you and your volunteers that have to live with the design of the counters, the location of the display cases, and location of the phone system.

The design for a new gift shop, will in most cases, will be determined and executed by an architect hired by the administration of the organization. Municipalities, knowing that there is profit in this type of shop, typically include an area for retail sales in the planning of zoos, parks and museums.

Even though, the volunteer group may not be a part of the initial planning, they may be able to decide on arrangement of fixtures in the shop. In either case it is a good idea for the volunteer organization that will be operating or manning the shop to submit a written list of suggestions that could be incorporated in the plans. It is your responsibility to make sure your ideas are translated into realities.

Again, I repeat - if no one asks, you should submit your list of ideas. This conveys to the host institution or facility that the volunteers have a vested interest in a successful outcome of the project assuring that the shop will accommodate the needs of the volunteers as well as the customer.

A designer, architect or administrator may have no idea of the requirements for the good design of such a shop. How many shops have you gone into and the square footage was not adequate, or the arrangement of the shop was not appropriate, or it was not wheelchair accessible or the check-out counter was in a dark corner in the back of the shop? Think about what your "perfect" shop should look like, what features it will offer, and where everything will be placed. Visit other shops in your area to get ideas. Pay special attention to gift shops you see in airports, hospitals, museums and any other public location. Write down what works, what doesn't, and how you would make improvements. Have other volunteers do the same. Input from a group that has had actual experience or has done in-depth investigating is what makes a workable shop.

Include in your list a visible location for the shop, realistic square footage for the shop, office or workroom and a storage area for the shop inventory. Ideas for display windows, and the front entrance; also important aspects of the shop, should be listed. Include suggestions for necessary plumbing and electrical connections/requirements, grid/slat wall areas to hang or display merchandise, and finally a security system. To help, I've included some phone numbers and e-mail addresses of suppliers of fixtures and equipment in this chapter. Although I've used many of these suppliers, this information is not a recommendation or endorsement of any company or supplier, but rather a starting place for you.

SELECTING (OR CHANGING) A LOCATION

Another key to success and achieving your goals is the shop's location! You've probably heard the old saying in the commercial real-estate business that goes something like this, "The three most important elements for a successful business are **location, location, location.**"

Think about this: have you ever gone to a museum, and the exit was through the gift shop? But this idea is not just used in museum shops. If you've ever flown from Canada to the U.S. through Vancouver, you must go through customs. But that's not all you MUST go thru. As you get your passport stamped at the customs counter, you must exit through a huge Canadian gift shop. Believe me when I say more than one traveler leaving Canada has thought, "well, I guess I should buy a few gifts for my friends."

As the saying goes - location, location, location is important, important, important! Architects were thinking location, location, location when designing the above mentioned gift shops locations. And your architect or designer should have the same thing in mind. So start thinking about your shop. Is it by an entrance or exit of the building? If not, could your organization consider remodeling?

Even though you may have a "captive audience" customer base, the shop should be easily accessible, clearly visible and strategically located. Perhaps in a hospital setting the shop would attract more customers if the location were near the entrance, rather than an exit as in the case of a museum or other souvenir type shops. With a strategic location you have a monopoly on the visitors.

What if you can't do anything about your location? Here are a few ideas to bring the customer to your door:

✓ A display case placed near the entrance or exit, displaying intriguing items for sale in the shop. Include directions to the shop
✓ A small kiosk or cart near the entrance or exit, with attendant to sell small necessities or souvenirs and to give directions to shop
✓ A map of the building at the entrance, showing the location of the gift shop, prominently highlighting the easiest route to get there
✓ Promotions, advertising suggestion in Chapter 12

BUILDING, REMODELING OR EXPANDING

Whether your organization is starting from scratch or thinking about expansion or remodeling you must take steps to achieve a near perfect floor plan with all the trimmings. Your organization may have a small make shift shop or your shop might have spilled over onto carts or kiosks, signaling a need for expansion. Or your organization may be in the process of expansion and a new gift shop is in the plans.

Regardless of whether you are building new or renovating, where do you start? With a budget of course, just like any project! After you have a clear idea of the space required, the fixtures and equipment you need, and the special features you want to incorporate, you're ready to make a budget.

To refresh your memory, you might review Chapter 3, where budgeting for building and remodeling is discussed. Since this aspect will involve the administration of the host institution or facility, the building superintendent, a building or remodeling contractor; realize you will need plenty of input from your organization, and that the more information you've researched and presented in written form the better. You will need a lot of ammunition to get your points across.

If you're in a position many shops find themselves in, you may need to compromise to get the administration to agree to give up space to expand or build a new shop. And to persuade the powers that be, you must present this need in a professional manner to get results. The following suggestions are 'sure fire' ways to attract their attention and ones I've used within two other facilities to expand relatively small gift shop spaces.

Sure Fire Methods of Persuasion

Persuasion is a skill you'll need to master. And the first method I typically use is a letter in the form of a proposal. The letter should be written by the board of directors of the volunteer organization. This is the best way to approach this subject.

However, before you fire off a letter outlining your proposal, do a survey of your customer base and have the board of your organization or an appointed committee investigate possible ways to expand or remodel your shop in a way that can best serve your clientele.

The survey should include questions on type of merchandise the customer would purchase in the new shop, including merchandise that would add to the convenience of the employee or visitor customer. And the questionnaire should address the visibility and accessibility of the existing shop and improvements for expansion, highlighting where customers perceive deficiencies. Incorporate the results of this survey in the letter.

Include in this letter the prime location for the shop and a brief explanation. For example a shop tucked back in of a hospital may better serve its clients near the entrance, close to the coffee shop or next to the newborn nursery. A gift shop located in a museum within a busy downtown location may want to position the gift shop closer to the street exit.

Address in your proposal letter the question on how customers would be better served by a new shop or remodeling and note how at present, because of a lack of space, sales are less than what they could be. For example, you may attract more customers if you offered lay-a-way services and had room for storing the items purchased, or during the holiday season how you may be able to attract more business if you had a work area for gift wrapping.

When researching the information for the proposal, the committee should examine, and then answer the following questions within the proposal:

1. The square footage in the existing shop and proposed square footage for expansion.

2. Annual gross sales per square foot, in dollars and cents, now compared to how the increase in square footage could increase sales.

3. Provide a proposed preliminary sketch of a floor plan, and if possible the estimated cost for expansion.

Present the proposal in a straightforward business like manner, including the above suggested information. Make a request to schedule a planning meeting.

To help get you started, on the next page, I've included an example of a proposal letter.

With proper planning, you could redesign the shop for maximum benefit, getting you started on your way to achieving your goals of making profit for your non-profit gift shop!

PROPOSAL LETTER

Volunteer Organization
Address

Month 00, 200_

Administration
Address

Dear Administrator,
The Volunteer Organization's Gift Shop needs additional space to better serve our customers. The customer base consists of the employees and visitors of

_____.

Our gross sales for the past fiscal year were $_____. Annual sales per square foot were $_____. The proposed addition to the shop could increase the sales by $_____. This would increase our annual gift to

_____by $_____.

The square footage of the existing shop is _____. The volunteer organization proposes that the shop's floor space be increased to _____. We suggest that the _____wall of the shop be moved out ____feet into the Lobby area. This space in the Lobby, not being utilized at the present time, would add approximately _____square feet of selling space besides adding to the needed storage area.

This expansion would make the shop wheelchair accessible, this addition would, also, provide a more convenient and attractive place for the visitors and employees to shop.

The potential for increased sales and service is tremendous.

Enclosed is a preliminary sketch of the proposed addition and the results of a recent survey supporting the needed expansion.

Looking forward to meeting with the administration to discuss this proposal.

Sincerely,

Volunteer President

Enclosure

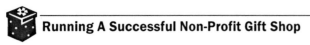

DESIGNING THE FLOOR PLAN

Whether you're remodeling, renovating, creating a new shop, or simply reevaluating the existing layout of your shop, the next logical step is designing a floor plan. The floor plan of a successful shop should be not only pleasing to the eye but also workable and safe for the customer as well as the volunteer or attendant working in the shop. And remember, it should accommodate wheelchair customers.

The average square footage of most gift shops within a hospital setting is approximately 465 square feet. The size of a shop in a municipal surrounding is usually somewhat larger. So I've elected to give you a few examples, based on the average hospital shop. But regardless of the size, the design principles and suggestions can be applied to any shop.

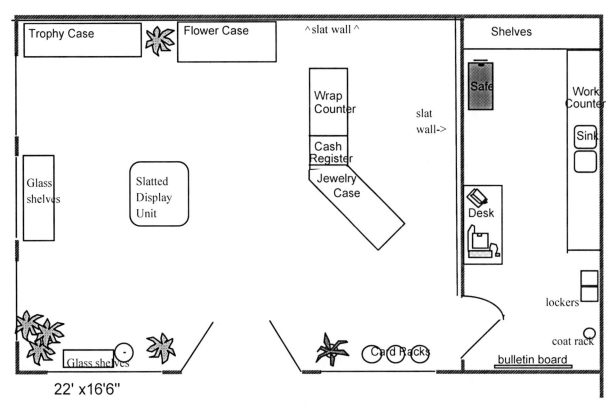

A gift shop floor plan (400 square feet)

Notice in the floor plan example, that the window areas make a nice backdrop for displays, the merchandise can be seen from both inside and out. The use of windows, in the plan, not only attracts the customer's attention with displays but also serves as deterrent for shoplifting and theft, providing visibility.

The workroom, which I think is a necessity in any shop, ideally has a sink, counter workspace, storage shelves, safe, bulletin board, lockers, desk and computer equipment.

When arranging the fixtures in the shop, the convenience of the volunteer attending the shop should be a top priority. Volunteers need to see the customers, should be able to move around behind display cases, and not work in fear of falling objects. There are no blocked or 'bottlenecked' areas leaving way for a safe exit in case of an emergency. In other words the shop should be a safe environment. Notice in the floor plan that the shop attendant can exit from either side of the counter, providing quick access to merchandise and attending customers.

The layout of the shop also has provided ample room for the wheelchair customers. The entrance to the shop should be 36 inches wide to accommodate a wheelchair. Most doors in modern buildings meet this requirement. Include in the planning committee a person that uses a wheelchair. Their input is invaluable.

Note: When doing the planning don't forget the door hardware, providing access to the shop. Many people with mobility disabilities and others with a disability that limits grasping, such as arthritis, find some types of handle difficult or impossible to use. Door hardware, such as a round door knob (which requires tight grasping and twisting to operate) or a handle with a thumb latch are also inaccessible and must be modified or replaced, if doing so is readily achievable.

Changing or adding door hardware is usually relatively easy and inexpensive. A round doorknob can be replaced with a lever handle or modified by adding a clamp-on lever. In some cases, a thumb latch can be disabled so the door can be pulled open without depressing the latch or the hardware may be replaced. A flat panel-type pull handle can be replaced with a loop-type handle. A lever handle is accessible because it can be operated without tight grasping, pinching or twisting.

Back to the floor plan, notice that the cash register counter looks out on the rest of the shop and the workroom is easily accessible in case the volunteers need to wrap a package or go in the back to get more inventory. All tall display cases are against the wall and there are no tall cases or counters blocking the vision of the shop or towering over the volunteers. The shop attendant's vision of the entire shop will help discourage shoplifting. This is a typical method used in many convenience stores.

Let me give you an example of why this is so important. Recently, in my area, a local hospital expanded and constructed a large area at the front entrance for the volunteer's gift shop. They hired architects and design planners but did not consult with the volunteer organization that would be manning the shop.

The volunteers, while, elated with the beautiful brand new shop, knew that the tall display cases designed for the center of the shop, blocked visibility. Worse yet, after the shop was opened the cases did indeed prove to be unworkable, and had to be replaced by lower displays that provided visibility throughout the shop. This added to the cost, which meant money that could have been better spent was used to fix what should have been considered in the first place. This is another reason the input of the volunteer actually manning the shop is so important.

And a fellow volunteer related this story to me at a recent volunteer conference. The gift shop in the new hospital in her town was beautiful. It even had a coffee and juice bar and a fireplace for atmosphere, but the counter under the only phone in the shop was 48 inches deep making it almost impossible to reach the wall phone which had been installed high above the counter. No one thought about this important detail in the plan! (The volunteers were not included in the planning)

Another item to consider when designing your plan is the checkout area. The checkout area should be near the entrance and/or exit of the shop, as in the example. In many existing gift shops, this area is often hidden at the back of the shop, making it inconvenient for the customer, unworkable for the attendant, not to mention, making it easier for shoplifters to get away undetected.

FIXTURES

While the plans are being finalized for construction or remodeling of the gift shop, you should start thinking about the fixtures, display cases and accessories needed. A good way to get some ideas is again to do what you've done before - visit some of the retail gift shops in your area shopping centers and inquire about their display cases. Explain about your volunteer organization and the proposed shop and see if the shop owners have any recommendations on what works and what doesn't. And who knows, maybe you'll expand your circle of volunteers in the process. I know of one volunteer manager that did just that, and the owner of a local retail gift shop offered to help set up the volunteer operated shop. This retail shop owner was someone who was unaware of the volunteer organization and once involved proved to be a valuable resource. After the shop was up and running, the shop owner even volunteered her time as an advisor to the volunteer operated shop.

Contact other volunteer shop managers and ask for information on purchasing fixtures. Who knows? They just might have an old case, which would be perfect for your shop, sitting in their storeroom. Many shops that have upgrading their cases would be glad to get rid of used fixtures, especially if you 'cart them off'. You will learn a lot talking with other managers of non-profit gift shops. Probably the most valuable information that will come from these meetings is you will learn from their mistakes.

Next, look in the yellow pages of your local phone book under "shop fixtures". And don't forget the Internet. Use your favorite search engine to type in keywords such as 'Retail Display Cases'. You'll find plenty of listings.

Two of the best websites I've found for fixtures are Acme Display.com (888-305-8907) in Los Angeles, California and Display-Showcases.com (800-868-2013) in Kansas City, Missouri.(I've included 800 numbers in case you do not have access to the Internet.)

Another company to order a catalog from is Fixtures International in Houston, Texas, 800-444-1253. These sites have a limited catalog on line, plus the ability to order a complete catalog right on the web page. Or if you aren't connected, just dial their 800 number and request a catalog. On-line sites with a lot of information are: http://www.discountshelving.com and http://www.nu-era.com.

With an Internet connection, you could purchase all fixtures and equipment needed for the shop on-line, without leaving the comfort of your desk. But even though I'm Internet savvy, I'd rather do it the traditional way – in person. I think seeing the real thing and talking to real people will generate and spark ideas that will ultimately lead to the perfect shop. I use the Internet for the technical details, and to compare prices, then I pay a visit to a couple of local fixture warehouses.

The on-line information also makes it easy to work with a committee and other in your organization. They will be able to look at the many fixture choices right from the comfort of home. Then you can correspond by email with your information.

When purchasing fixtures online or in person, you can choose from three different types of fixtures: custom, ready made or used fixtures. Used fixtures will save you money, and custom fixtures will of course cost more but will better match your space and décor. So the only way to really decide is to have the planning committee or gift shop staff allocate an amount that is reasonable for your organization to spend, and then work from there. Again the magic of the budget usually helps you decide what is best for the shop overall.

Fixtures to Buy

Start with the most important fixture, the wrap counter that will house the cash drawer/register. After reviewing your floor design plans, visualize where the counter will be located and just what type of counter will best fit in your plan. For example, you can choose from a single register counter with shelves and no frills, or a counter with a register well, bag slots and cash drawer. Or you might decide on a counter with writing ledge, bag slots, cash drawer and shelves. There are plenty of options to choose from, so don't skimp on features but don't go over budget.

In some cases, the fixtures can be custom designed for your shop for the same price as some ready-made counters. Most suppliers of shop fixtures have designers that can plan a layout for your shop if you have not already done so. They are glad to work with the architect/builder and can design and have their craftsmen build anything from a sit-down jewelry display case with Queen Anne style legs, to a unique mahogany display pedestal. The designer should make a visit to the shop or the proposed site before starting the plan to confer with the architect. There is usually a cost for this service or it might be included in the price of the custom made displays and fixtures.

Whatever style you choose, from antique, avant-garde, art deco, modern or traditional, make sure that you are communicating the needs of the shop and that the designer understands those needs. If you can, sketch an example of the counter or take a photo of a counter you saw in a local shop that you think might work in your shop. Remember that custom designed fixtures will require additional time for construction so be sure to allow for this in your opening schedule.

If you have a limited budget, like most shops, you can design the shop with ready made or used fixtures and display cases and still have that custom look. With a fixture/display catalog, the shop's floor plan, a ruler, pencil, calculator and a few long hours, you can design a workable layout of fixtures for the shop. Then, when you walk into the fixture store, the designer or salesmen will evaluate your plan and suggest ready-made standard fixtures and displays they have in stock that will work with your design.

One thing to keep in mind, all fixtures should be purchased for the most display space that can be achieved. The fixtures should compliment the shop and at the same time be convenient for the volunteer sales staff. For example, the jewelry case in the shop should not have more than 2 display shelves within arms reach. If you purchase display cases with shelves near the floor they are out of the customers' range of vision, out of reach for the volunteer when assisting the customer and difficult when making a display. The lower portion of the case can be used for storage.

Think of how you will be displaying the merchandise and more importantly how the customer will see that merchandise. Will you carry apparel and need hanging racks? Will you need a locked case for valuable items? Will you need a refrigerated case for selling soft drinks or displaying fresh flowers? Will you need the safety of tempered glass display cases?

Since floor space in any shop is at a premium, every square inch should be utilized and the right fixtures can help you do just that. Racks hung from the ceiling to display T-shirts and other clothing items are a great way to maximize space as are chains or rope displays for hanging such things as plush animals. And slat or grid walls are convenient and economical ways to display merchandise. They offer a tremendous amount of versatility. I think that you will find that the slat wall will be easier to work with and provide more possibilities for displays because they accommodate and display almost any item.

But beware! Unless you have had experience with the accessories, connectors, hooks, shelves and brackets for the slat wall, I suggest that you get help from the supplier. Why? Because of its versatility, there are a wide variety of brackets and hooks and you could end up with a drawer full of useless brackets and hooks. What you need to know is the exact amount of slat wall space you have and the types of merchandise you want to display before you purchase the hooks and brackets.

Jewelry Cases

If your merchandise will include jewelry you will need a case. The jewelry case in the shop should not have more than 2 display shelves within arms reach. If you purchase display cases with display shelves near the floor they are out of the customers' range of vision, out of reach for the volunteer when assisting the customer and difficult when making a display. The lower portion of the case can be used for storage.

Below is an example of this type of case:

Jewelry Case

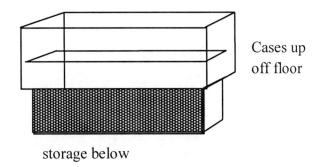

Cases up
off floor

storage below

Center Island Stand

The center island slat wall display is yet another retailer (as well as customer) friendly display you should consider incorporating into your shop. Display accessories for such cases are endless. And any kind of merchandise can be displayed making it easy for customers to see and touch the merchandise and for volunteers to stock the inventory. Everything from hanging items such as purses, hats, t-shirts to candy and gum can be displayed, and more importantly changed with ease at anytime.

Detailed below is an example of a Center Island Slat Wall. You've probably have seen them in airport gift shops where space is at a premium, and the ability to display lots of products from all sides is a must.

Center Island Slat Wall

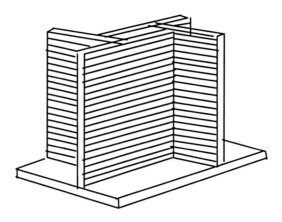

Shops considering selling perishable goods such as flowers or food items will require refrigerated display cases. These cases are typically used for floral sales or sales of cold drinks and snack foods. These cases can be custom designed or purchased in a standard size.

For more information on cases or to order one for your shop, call Floral Tech at 800-535-3295 or Floral Line at 800-239-3722. If you require a refrigerated case for food and soda pop, not just floral items, a good place to start to look for information on refrigerated cases is Artic Star of Texas, 800-229-6562. And don't over look this web site http://www.srcrefrigeration.com/ because, it too, has plenty of information on refrigerated cases for retail shops.

When choosing a refrigerated case of any kind, make sure you allow plenty of space for the location of the case in the shop, as typically they are larger than most other display cases. In addition, you also have to think about how the doors on the case will open, and whether you have enough clearance for the door to swing open. If not, a sliding door may be a better choice. When you order, you should make sure to specify you want a unit that does not require drainage otherwise provisions for a drain should be installed. Also make sure you have the proper electrical outlet accommodations.

Lighting

Don't forget that the lighting in your shop is also a fixture and a very important one! Lighting should be included in the planning stage. It is something that is often overlooked until after the shop is opened and then you discover that there is not enough light over the cash register or that the storeroom is dark. So plan ahead and when you do so, keep in mind the following in your floor plan:

- ✓ You will need ample lighting over the register counter
- ✓ You will need lighting to accent the window displays
- ✓ You will need overhead spot lights to highlight pedestals or table displays
- ✓ You will need lighting over the areas where magazines or books and greeting cards will be displayed
- ✓ You will need ample lighting in the storeroom or office

Note: When planning the lighting for the shop, especially if it is a small shop, be aware that lighting does create heat. Customers will not want to linger in a shop that is too warm.

Display Case Lighting

Remember that lighting in your display cases will accent and enhance your merchandise. Not only can light be installed in custom designed cases but in ready-made cases lighting is oftentimes included. I would recommend having lighted jewelry cases, lighted trophy type wall display cases. If you have older cases with no lighting, local stores such as Wal-Mart stock "under the counter" lighting that can easily be installed in older cases. Armed with a screwdriver you can install your own lighting in any case in no time.

After Hours Lighting

Another neglected lighting application is 'after hours' lighting, you know, the lighting you see when the place is closed. You may not be aware of the customer traffic that passes the shop when it's closed, but they are there. And they won't know you're there unless you have adequate outdoor and indoor lighting.

A strategically placed spot light highlighting a display in the front window of the shop attracts the attention of a passing potential customer enticing and persuading them to return during business hours. This type of lighting is especially needed if your shop is in hospital where visitors come and go at all hours of the day and night. You may be able to purchase outdoor and indoor after-hours lighting from the same company that provided you with the display fixtures. When shopping for after hour lighting, ask the salesperson to turn off the lights to see how the after-hours lighting will look, and make sure you check out how easy (or difficult) it is to replace bulbs.

So with your floor plan in hand, make appointments with some of the shop fixture and lighting suppliers in your area. Visit their showrooms. Make sure you get estimates from two or more companies to bring back to the board of your organization or planning committee for approval. And remember to ask about delivery charges and set up fees. You will want the fixture or lighting company to install or set up and position your counters once they are delivered because many may be too heavy for you to lift.

Also make sure they include any additional charges for delivery and setup in their proposal. Also find out how portable or transportable the cases are. There's no doubt you may end up rearranging things from time to time, and will need to clean, so the more portable or moveable they are, the better.

CHAPTER 7
Seventh Step: Selecting the Right Equipment

Setting up a shop and purchasing the necessary equipment can be a big expense. And it doesn't stop at just buying lighting fixtures and display cases. There are great many hidden expenses you'll run into, not to mention additional tools you'll need to run a successful shop. Since the machines to operate your shop will be costly, I will start out this chapter with suggestions to help you get an idea of how and where you can save a few dollars. Here are a few suggestions on how to obtain office and computer equipment at bargain prices:

✓ Contact a name brand dealer or leasing company to inquire about reconditioned equipment that carries a warranty. A dependable piece of equipment that can stand up to the everyday use by many different volunteers is needed. However, I don't suggest purchasing equipment at a close out or "as is" sale.

✓ Ask for donations. Many large companies, especially those that might be downsizing or going out of business in your area might have a warehouse full of good unused equipment that they would be glad to donate. Oftentimes companies upgrade computer systems simply because a new piece of software has hit the market, leaving perfectly good systems replaced. Such systems will not only work fine for the shop, but really are preferred since most of the bugs are worked out.

✓ Contact the purchasing department of the non-profit organization that you represent. They maybe able to get a better deal since they may have an account with a computer, fixture, or electrical company. Do your homework beforehand, so you will know exactly what you want when the purchase order is placed, and to minimize paperwork.

✓ Poll your membership for donations. People want to contribute.

> *A WORD OF WARNING! Make sure that when you accept used equipment it fits your needs, is not obsolete and that parts are still available. Although donations are always the preferable way to go, sometimes people are simply looking to off-load their junk on anybody willing to haul it off.*

After you "shop around" and have educated yourself on the type of equipment that will be best for the shop, compare prices from at least two sources to get the best deal. Also don't forget to shop the Internet. Sites such as Buy.com or AskSimon.com allow you to do side-by-side price comparisons. But don't forget. Any product's price you compare on the Internet must include shipping, the most expensive part of almost any product purchased over the Internet.

I always suggest any way possible that's legal for securing equipment and merchandise without depleting your funds. And most of this can be done by just asking. Ask for help. Ask for donations. Ask to see equipment that is headed out the door destine for another organization. Remember, the dollar you save will go to the philanthropic cause or project you are working towards. So, as with anything relating to non-profit organizations, be frugal! It's not about the money you spend, but about the money you retained for your cause.

OFFICE EQUIPMENT

The proper office equipment can save your time and the time of your volunteers, allowing you to do more and do it more professionally. Get the wrong stuff and you have nightmare after nightmare on your hands. The gift shop will need a calculator or adding machine, cash register, computer with the necessary accessories, and a purchased or lease credit card terminal, for starters. Two phone lines are essential for the shop, one that is connected with the main switch board of the organization, and the other line for credit card approval, check verification and long distance calls. An answering machine also necessary to handle after business hours calls.

Although by no means is the following a definitive guide to office equipment, I've included some tips from my own experience on what equipment is necessary. And again, I stress frugality here, but more importantly I also stress ease of use. Your volunteers may not be techno-savvy. So don't get sucked into the edict that you need the latest and greatest computer system. You don't. Most shops inventory can be kept on a simple spreadsheet, as can the books. Although it would be nice to have a computerized cash register, your shop may not do the volume of sales that would require it. And the most basic of all office products, the calculator often works better and quicker than any computer system.

CALCULATORS

The calculator is a shop's necessity. They are available in a wide range of models and prices. Make sure that the calculator you purchase for use in the shop is a ten-key model, prints out a tape, has at least an eight-digit capacity and is able to handle negative numbers. Also, purchase a couple of hand held calculators to position by the cash register.

COPY MACHINE

A reasonably priced copier should include useful features such as reduction and enlargement, zoom, photo mode and toner saver, plus multiple copying and be able to copy size: legal (8-1/2" x 14") to Business Card (2" x 3-1/2"). While most of the organizations where you volunteer will be happy for you to use their copy machines it is convenient to have one right in the shop if your budget permits. A good machine that will fit your needs in the shop should be around $500. If you purchase a scanner with your computer equipment, this could serve as a copier if your copying needs are minimal.

COMPUTER EQUIPMENT & SOFTWARE

A computer system, which typically is comprised of the central processing unit (or CPU) which is the brains, a monitor, keyboard, floppy disk drive, hard disk (your electronic file cabinet), printer and various software programs is an essential part of even the smallest of shop. Not only can you generate all business correspondence, enter and shop all financial data, but you can also use the computer for designing your own inexpensive advertising, including setting up a Web site. Also, now, with many accounting programs, you can tie the computer into your cash register and credit card terminal, thereby automating the entire purchasing and inventory process.

But before you invest in any computer equipment you should consider several factors first, as these will dictate what type of computer, software and additional devices you will need. The factors to consider include:

- ✓ Who will be using the system
- ✓ Their level of knowledge of computers
- ✓ The types of information you will be storing
- ✓ The tasks you want to automate
- ✓ Where the computer will be used/placed in the shop
- ✓ The security you need to employ to protect customer information

Once you know the exact types of activities the computer will be used for, where it will be used, and who is going to use it, the next step is to identify the best system for your needs. Experts agree that you should stick with well-known brands like Compaq, Apple, or Hewlett-Packard. Also top mail order vendors like Dell and Gateway are always a good choice as well. All offer advanced system features in prices that range from $500 to $2,000 depending upon the options you purchase. Most of the manufacturers offer at least a one-year limited warranty and many computer superstores provide additional warranty and repair options, which are recommended, particularly if they offer on-site repair.

NOTE: The easiest computer to use is the Apple Macintosh, commonly referred to as a Mac. The operating system is intuitive, much more so than Windows computers, and the system crashes (or stops working) far less than most Windows computers. If your needs include just simple word processing, spreadsheets, databases for inventory, and perhaps graphics programs to make signs, check into buying or getting a donation of a Mac. But remember there will be less support and fewer options.

Regardless of the actual brand you get, experts offer the following explanation for the options you'll need to pay attention to when buying a computer system:

CPU – The simplest recommendation? Get the fastest you can based on how much you have to spend. Don't get confused, since many of the smaller nuances in the processors matter little when you are simply writing letters, searching the Internet or entering information into a spreadsheet. The nuances are more for those heavy-duty users who play lots of games, work with graphic intensive software programs or do a lot of computer aided drafting.

So how do you know which is the best for you? It's really not that complicated. Let's start with the processor itself. Those computers that run the popular Microsoft Windows software run on either an AMD or Intel brand processor. Intel-based computers are typically more expensive than AMD, basically because you are paying for a "brand-name." And AMD processors typically run faster than Intel systems, typically at a cheaper price.

Both manufacturers offer a variety of chips, each running at different speeds. The speed of the computer is rated by the Gigahertz designation. What you should look for is the fastest speed. The larger the number, the faster the computer. So for example if you had to choose from one computer rated at 1.2 Gigahertz and another rated at 1.6 Gigahertz, the latter would be the faster of the two.

RAM – RAM stands for Random Access Memory and just as the processor is considered the engine of the computer, the RAM could best be compared to the top of your desk, your workspace so to speak. It's the place where the computer loads in the Web pages you're looking at, the letter you are writing and the instructions that keep the system connected to your printer. As with any desk, the larger the desktop, the more paperwork you can pile on top of it. So it goes with RAM; the larger the amount of RAM, the more programs and files you can work on while the system is on. RAM is sold in Megabytes and Gigabytes. A gigabyte is larger than a megabyte, and the more of either you have, the more you'll be able to work with at one time and faster your computer will respond. A system with at least 256MB is a very workable system, especially these days with computer programs being so complex.

Hard Drive - The hard drive is the computer's long-term data storage or if we continue with the desk analogy, the hard drive is like your file cabinet. Where the RAM is the top of your desk, you need some place to permanently shop all the files you work on and that's just what the hard drive is for. And with anything relating to computers, the bigger the better. Look for something between 20 and 60GB (gigabytes).

Other Types of Drives – Aside from the hard drive, which is an internal device stored in the same box that also houses the CPU and the various computer connectors, almost every computer comes two other types of drives – a floppy drive and a CD-ROM drive. Again, the same premise is used with all other computer components – the bigger or faster, the better. The standard floppy drive accommodates a removable 3.5-inch diskette that can hold 1.44MB of information. That's a lot of letters, memos, or price sheets, but not a lot of digital pictures, music or computer programs. So typically you use the floppy drive to back up small amounts of information, copy files so you can take them home and work with them, or transfer information to other computers when the computers aren't connected to a network or the Internet.

Unlike floppy drives, CD-ROM drives come in a variety of configurations and hold about 600 times more than a standard floppy drive, or about 650MB. Since all CD-ROM drives hold the same amount of information, the major difference between one and another is the speed at which they bring up the information stored on them.

The speeds are typically rated like this: 4X, 8X, 46X and so on, meaning if the drive is rated as a 16X drive, it's 16 times faster than the original CD-ROM drive that was first manufactured. So again, the higher the number, the faster the drive will pull up the information stored on the CD disc.

Another variance in CD-ROM drives is whether the drive has the capability to write information to a disc. Traditionally CD-ROM drives simple READ information off a disc, and cannot write to the disk, unlike floppy drives. However, newer, CD-R/W drives can write to special blank CD-ROM discs you can buy in just about any computer shop for pennies a disc. The experts recommend buying a computer with a built-in CD-R/W drive so you can use it to backup almost your entire hard drive to a single disc.

Monitor – Again, the theory goes - the bigger the better. But with this option, I strongly encourage you to look before you buy since you and your employees may be staring at the monitor for hours on end. Most experts agree a 17-inch monitor is preferred, particularly if you plan on viewing multiple document and spreadsheets all at the same time. Flat-panel LCD displays save on space and are easier on the eyes, but they typically run about $300 more than the larger, bulkier standard monitors. In a small gift shop, with limited counter space, a flat-panel monitor will be worth the additional money in the space it saves. But again, the experts caution you actually see the monitor in action before you buy. Flat-panel displays vary greatly in quality, clarity and brightness and what may look good to one person, may be out of focus or too dark to another.

Printers – The printer you purchase will depend on what you plan to do with the printer. These days you can use most printers to print not only sales receipts, but also banners, iron-on T-shirt transfers, thank-you cards, photos and more. So before you buy that printer, sit down and consider what kinds of forms, marketing material, and other printed matter you plan to do on your own, as opposed to outsourcing to a printing firm like Kinko's.

For example, many gift shop owners prefer to use a pre-printed duplicate invoice or receipt where the invoice or receipt is printed on carbon-copy paper and one copy is given to the customer and the other kept by the gift shop. For this type of system where you are using pre-printed duplicate sales receipts, you need an impact printer like a dot-matrix or the less-popular daisy wheel printer since these are the only printers that make an impact hard enough to print through the carbon-less paper.

If you haven't already purchased or don't plan to purchase pre-printed duplicate sales receipts or other forms, you can simply use blank paper as sales receipts or invoices. In that case, you don't need a printer that makes an impact, and instead can use any type of ink jet printer. These printers print by literally spraying the ink onto the page, and can also print in color. Plus many ink jet printers these days are not only extremely cheap, but also can print photo quality prints. The experts recommend ink jet printers mainly because of their price and versatility. But when buying a printer don't just base your decision on price. Instead check to see how long the ink jet cartridges that hold the ink last. Although the printer may be cheap, the cartridges may not last very long and may cost as much if not more than the printer itself. This is especially important if you plan on print a great deal of flyers, signs and brochures on your own.

Modems for Faxing and the Internet – Whatever computer you purchase, make sure it comes with both a fax modem and a network connection called an Ethernet or 10/100 Base-T connector. The fax modem can be used to fax correspondence, price lists, sales flyers and more to vendors and customers, plus receive faxes from others. Plus fax modems can also connect you to the Internet via a phone line. If you plan on being on the Internet all the time, or plan on using your fax modem capabilities frequently, you will need to install a separate phone line in your shop. However, if you don't plan on faxing much or have no plans to connect to the Internet, you can use your main phone line or the phone line connected to your credit card machine.

However, if you don't want tie up a line or wait for web pages to load, there is another option. You can use an Ethernet 10/100 Base-T connector to connect to faster cable, satellite or DSL modems that send information from 50 to 100 times quicker than a modem would and don't use the phone line to do it. Instead these types of Internet connections either use the cable TV-hookup, satellite connections or in the case of DSL your existing phone line without interrupting your phone calls. But unlike modems, not all computers come with network connections, so you must ask to ensure this is included with the system if you plan to use these high-speed Internet connections.

Scanner – Although it may sound like a luxury item, a scanner is a great addition to any system. Why? With a scanner, you can use it scan in pictures, product catalogs, drawings, and more that you can then put into newsletters, sales flyers, signs and more. (Just be careful that you don't violate copyright laws by scanning in artwork or printed materials you don't have authorization to reproduce.). You can also use it as a cheap copy machine to make a few copies, or used in conjunction with your fax modem to scan, then fax printed documents.

The features you want in a scanner again are the same as with any computer product – the more the better. 32-bit scanners are better than 24-bit scanners and 600 dots per inch are better than 300 dots per inch. A good scanner is typically a flat-bed scanner that allows you to place books and magazines on top of the scanning glass. It would offer 48-bit scanning with a resolution of from 2400 to 4800 dots per inch. It would offer 32 to 48-bit color and would come with a USB connector and cable to connect to the computer. If you plan on scanning slides or other such material you should also look for a slide-adapter for the scanner. If you plan on scanning a great deal of single pages, you should also look for an optional sheet-feeder that will automatically feed pages through the scanner like copy machines do.

Software - There is a program on the market designed especially for volunteer operated shops and organizations. As expected this program does not come cheap, so most shops are using the program Quick Books for accounting. This is an easy program that will generate all your financial statements and do the inventory.

Buying Recommendations:

Buying a computer may be a confusing and exasperating experience. There are so many options. If you do not have the knowledge or expertise to make an intelligent decision on the purchase of a computer and all the necessary equipment, then form a committee of three or four of your most computer knowledgeable people in your organization. Have each go to a different computer shop to collect prices and information about products and services offered. Then have them return with all the information they've gathered. But be careful to look at the fine print on many of the offers major computer vendors advertise. Many outline great prices, but only after mail-in rebates, while others require you sign-up for a year or more of Internet service before you get the discounted price. Another option is to use the Internet to comparison shop. Web sites such as MySimon.com or Buy.com help you compare not only prices but also features. Also make sure you check recent publications like Consumer Reports for rating and recommendations on the latest computer hardware. And sites such as www.cnet.com and www.pcworld.com routinely offer yearly reviews of the best computers systems available.

CASH REGISTER

Cash register or cash drawer is for transacting and recording sales and holding money needed for transactions. Any shop with anticipated sales of $40,000 or more a year should purchase a register that gives daily totals and generates reports on items sold. Sales tax computation, the date, item category and the discounted percentages should be able to be programmed in the machine.

A good place to start looking is at your local office Supply Company or log on to www.cashregistershop.com. Cash register companies will be glad to visit your shop to recommend registers and equipment needed for operations. Ask for written estimates, type of service and warrantees.

Shop with annual sales over $75,000 should consider a register with a scanner and built in credit card terminal or investing in a Point of Sale System (POS).

POINT OF SALE SYSTEM (POS)

"Point of Sale" is a completely automated retail management system that can be used to replace electronic cash registers.

POS is a much faster, more flexible means of entering sales and controlling inventory than a cash registers. The system offers far more capabilities than the traditional cash register and is also much easier to use. The POS program drives an interactive cash drawer, receipt printer, bar code scanner, shopper display unit, and magnetic card stripe reader.

Replacing stand-alone cash registers or separate retail software, it empowers you with all the audit trails needed for end-of-day reports. In addition, the system enables immediate and current inventory information so you will know what and when to reorder. The system allows capture of all customer information making for improved service. It offers integrated credit card processing, which means you don't have to re-key accounting or credit card information, and permits flexible product pricing configuration with checks to prevent selling at lower than designated price.

If your shop is interested in a POS, you will need to do research on the type of system best suited for your shop. There are many POS systems just designed for the small retailer. Again this is a good time to enlist the advice of other shop managers. This will be a large investment for the shop. Costs range anywhere from $2000 to over $10,000, so you can see why you need to do the research.

Following are web sites that cater to POS systems:

- ✓ www.cancommerce.com
- ✓ www.retailpro.com
- ✓ www.comcashpos.com
- ✓ www.runit.com

CHAPTER 8

Eighth Step: Understanding the Customer

The most important component of a business is your customer. Without the customer there is no business and no profit. So you must identify your customer. Who will come into the shop? What type of merchandise will they want or need to purchase? What services will they expect? This is called 'targeting'.

TARGETING

Even before you make your first merchandise purchase you need to target your customer. To do that, you must identify the types of shopper that will enter the gift shop and categorize the types of merchandise they will want to buy. Your immediate customer base may be comprised of visitors, patrons, tourists, patients, employees of the institution or facility in which the shop is located and volunteers of the organization - your "captive" customers. They will be your first priority, the people you will want to purchase merchandise for, the people you will want to serve.

One way to identify the customer is to compile a simple questionnaire that gives the customers the ability to voice their opinions on what they expect from the shop. To assure that you will get a response to the questionnaire, give an incentive such as 10% discount on a purchase, if they complete the questionnaire. This questionnaire could be made available in waiting areas or stuffed into the shopper's bag at the time of a purchase. It could be distributed with newsletters or other information to the volunteers and employees of the organization, facility or institution. The questions should address the convenience of the shop's hours, the type of merchandise desired and price range. Also ask what special services the shop could offer such as gift-wrapping, delivery, personal shopping, employee discounts, etc.

Such a survey/questionnaire is similar to those customer service surveys you may see in hotels. A customer that may find fault with your shop will probably be eager to fill out such a survey. And that's good! You need to know what you are doing right, but more importantly, you need to know what you are doing wrong.

The questionnaire will not only give you an idea of who enters the shop, but you also provide you with names and addresses, phone numbers and email addresses, creating an instant customer list to use later for advertisement. Plus, it will provide an avenue to stay in touch with your most important resource – the customer.

> **REMEMBER**: Don't just assume you serve only one group. You can broaden your customer base by attracting customers outside the immediate environment. Suggestions for specific way to reach outside customers are in the Chapter 12 "Promoting Business".

CUSTOMER SERVICE

Even though your gift shop may not depend on repeat business, customer service is important for public relations of your organization. Superior customer service will enhance the image of your non-profit organization besides increasing your business. The foundation of all retail business is service and service is even more important in this type of shop. Shop managers have found that the strongest selling point and the assurance of repeat customers is customer service. Provide the customer with individual and personalized service and they will be back to buy again. A recent survey conducted by Gifts & Decorative Accessories showed that successful shops had one thing in common... unique personal customer service.

Remember, since you are a volunteer operated business, the customer expects extra attention. All the volunteers and attendants working in the shop should be trained in providing a caring image and good customer service. The service, as well as the merchandise, should be exceptional!

Since shops located within a large business or organization have a built-in customer base with patrons, clients, visitors and employees, the shop should focus on service and offer a diversified product mix customized to this built-in customer base. For example, offering merchandise not readily available elsewhere is just another form of customer service.

As the baby boomer generation approaches retirement, increasing volume in the tourist business will result in increased business for museum, park and zoo gift shops. Also, as the population grows older, the hospital gift shop business will continue to grow with more patients and visitors. This means your shop should provide the customer personal attention - something large department and discount shops cannot do. Let's examine how to give that extra level of customer service.

How to Provide Good Customer Service

A good place to start is to instruct the volunteers or shop attendant in providing customer service. This instruction should start with phone etiquette. Suggest that they smile when answering the phone; this instantly puts the volunteer in a good mood and actually makes the volunteer sound friendlier over the phone. Also advise them to always have pad and pencil by the phone so they can write down any important information the customer may relay. Make sure you emphasize the importance of treating each caller with respect, even if the caller is complaining or seems unreasonable. The best advice you can give to the volunteer working in the shop is to always listen to the customer, whether on the phone or in person And keep reinforcing to all volunteers, that it's the customer that ultimately provides your profits that turns into the funds for your philanthropic projects.

Speaking of phone etiquette reminds me to remind you to use an answering machine after business hours or when no one is available to answer calls. This is another form of customer service. Also, don't think of an answering machine as just for after hours use. The answering machine could answer calls when the shop is manned by only one person, or if all the shop attendants are busy with customers. Make sure you purchase an answering machine that allows you to quickly choose more than one outgoing message. That way you can record a message for after hours, and then easily switch to another message during normal business hours when the attendants are preoccupied with shop customers. The messages should include the business hours, and pertinent information for the phone customer, like upcoming sale dates or special merchandise, plus the reason why the machine is taking the call in the first place (i.e. 'We're busy helping customers, but don't want to miss your call...'). In every message, encourage the caller to leave their name and number, the date and time they called, and the reason for the call, then make sure their call is returned as soon as possible.

Another way to serve the customer is with delivery, mailing or shipping services. If you provide delivery or shipping, make sure it is prompt and efficient. If you use order forms, with shipping instructions, make sure that the forms are simple and straightforward, that a child could follow the instructions. This will speed up the process and eliminate errors. If you take special orders for merchandise, it is advisable to have someone take full responsibility for the placement and delivery of the orders. That way this single point of contact will be able to handle any problems quickly, since they will know where to look for the order and shipping information.

And while you're ringing up that sale, listen to your customer's likes and dislikes, their requests and complaints. They are giving you a view from the other side of the counter that will suggest areas in which you can improve. Try to train the volunteer attendant to be attuned to these needs of the individual customer. Keep a blank journal for those volunteers to write down customer suggestions or complaints.

Other forms of customer service are to provide personal shopping service, phone order service, lay-a-ways, personalized gift baskets, gift wrapping and postal supplies.

A note about gift wrapping - the service of gift wrapping has become extremely popular as today's customer is more aware of presentation and design. The wrap, to **some** customers, is almost as important as the gift itself. Many people do not mind spending money to make sure the gift wrap is personalized. Just another way customer service increases sales! So provide training to your volunteers or attendants on the proper way to gift wrap.

Providing the above services will assure sales. But, this is the pleasant part of customer service; there is another side of customer service we should address. In dealing with the public, there are times when you will not be able to please a customer or a misunderstanding will occur between the customer and the shop management. **the customer complaint**. Addressing these complaints is just another form of customer service and handling them in a proper manner is good customer service.

Good customer service also means good communications. Provide your customer with all available information they need to do business with you successfully. Let them know about the shop's policies on returns, lay-a-ways, and refunds.

Do that **BEFORE** the sale so they will not be disappointed or expect something other than what you can provide. Make sure that your policies are posted in the shop. Make sure your major policies for returns, refunds and exchanges are written on the receipt and the customer is informed that a receipt is needed for these transactions. (If you choose to make this a policy in your shop)

Even when you have taken the precautions to prevent misunderstanding, they will occur. When a customer complains, immediately try to resolve the problem. Start off by letting the customer know that you **WILL** resolve the problem to their satisfaction and if you can't, you will find the person who can. This approach usually has a calming effect on the customer. Don't give them the runaround or accuse them of any wrongdoing.

Then give them clear information on how and when the issue will be resolved. Is the old saying 'the customer is always right", true? Of course not, but every customer should be made to feel they are right. Offer suggestions for a solution. Don't place blame, just stay focused on a solution. Those who may want to take advantage of your quality customer attitude will be few and far between. Most people are simply looking for a fair deal and to be treated with respect.

There is no more potential for a volatile situation than in the area of returns, especially when policies aren't followed. Make sure that all the volunteers know how to administer the return policy properly. And don't let them deviate for any reason. If they do, other customers will find out, and want to know why they don't get the same treatment. So follow your set policies. This establishes good customer relations and lets your customers know they can expect consistency in the way your volunteers deal with customers. Remember, communication is the ultimate form of customer service. Make sure that your volunteer or shop attendant understands all policies and procedures adopted by the shop and that they feel confident that they will have no trouble enforcing them.

Only when policies and procedures are not 'in place' would a customer have the opportunity to take unfair advantage. Without established guidelines, not only will there be chaos but it will lead to a customer's feeling of resentment and discrimination - that there are no real policies in place, only personal preferences. This will create a loss of respect from your customers and the volunteers which will ultimately affect sales in the shop. So always deal with everyone in the same way, giving everyone the same deal or resolution. Policies and procedures assure this will happen.

> **REMEMBER**: The best advertising is by word of mouth and news of good customer service will travel fast. Resolving customer problems and providing outstanding customer service will result in advertisement that "money can't buy".

Since most of the attendants in the shop are volunteers, they are expected to go that extra mile. Again, this is the only way you can effectively compete with the large department or discount shops. Providing services to your customer will assure that you will have a repeat customer or customer referral. But how do you go that extra mile? Here are some suggestions of services that "go that extra mile":

- Provide free gift-wrapping or charge a nominal fee.
- Provide free delivery service within a ten-mile radius.
- Provide phone order service.
- Provide mailing service for purchases.
- Provide shopping services.

All of these extra services will create more volunteer jobs. The more volunteers involved in your organization, the more the word will spread about your shop, and the more customers are likely to come to the gift shop. And remember, without customers, there's no way to insure achieving the goals set for the shop.

Customer Service Supplies

One thing you should stock in your shop is what I call "customer service supply inventory" and it's definitely a necessary part of your inventory. It is the inventory that keeps the shop running smoothly. Exactly what am I talking about? I'm talking about merchandise such as bags, gift boxes and wrapping paper. And you purchase these just like the gift merchandise, in a showroom at a major market, through catalogs and vendors. An easy way to order these supplies is through the Internet.

Just type in the words "gift wrap" and your search will bring up a number of companies. You can place an order on line, with no minimum and next day shipping. To add a special touch, you could have stickers printed with the name of the shop. These could be put on gift boxes, gift-wrapped packages or selected merchandise. Merchandise bags could, also, be imprinted with the name of the shop or host organization.

Other supplies, that are necessary to run the shop and accommodate the customer, are items such as note pads for jotting down those important phone messages from customers, pencils, pens, sales slips, adding machine and cash register tape, credit card supplies. Office supplies and shop supplies can be purchased through your local office supply shop, Sam's or Costco. Shop around for the best prices. Credit card supplies will be purchased through the company providing the service. You can also find great deals at close-out shops and dollar shops where oftentimes office supplies are in abundance for very cheap prices

CHAPTER 9
Ninth Step: Inventory – The Ins & Outs

Now we get to the fun part - buying!

It is a good idea to have more than one person doing the buying. You should appoint or solicit a group of buyers. Having more than one buyer assures that the merchandise will be diversified and you will have appealing merchandise for all customers. It provides sort of a check and balance system for purchasing. The buying duties should be divided into different departments and a buyer or buyers selected for each different category of merchandise sold in the shop.

You may think that within your organization there isn't anyone with that type of experience, but just think for a minute - you have experienced buyers all around you. Most of the members in your group, like yourself, have made purchases for a family for years. What better experience could you ask for! Your potential buyers have had to budget and purchase all types of merchandise for many years, for all sorts of people, in all sorts of circumstances. And now you could tap that knowledge and have them transfer their experience to shopping for items for the gift shop. With a few tips, you can turn those average consumers disguised as volunteers into savvy experienced gift shop buyers. In the last chapter you identified your customer, so make a list of all the items that this identified customer might purchase in your shop.

Remember, even though you have an advantage over regular retail gift shops – the prime location, a captive audience, (customer), with an incentive to buy; you may not get sales. Without the right merchandise they will not have the incentive to visit your shop and make that purchase. So put some thought into what type of merchandise you should purchase for resale in the shop.

If the shop is in a hospital setting, you will want to first identify what type of patient comes to the hospital. If the hospital has a large number of births, then you will want to purchase items for new babies and mothers. If the hospital does out-patient surgery, you will want to have, on hand, items for waiting visitors, impulse gift items for the patient and supplies needed for recovery at home. If the gift shop is in a museum, the purchases will be geared to the type of museum. If the shop is in a municipal park setting, you will want to carry souvenirs type merchandise. If the shop is in a zoo or animal park setting, any type of gifts pertaining to animals or nature, or crafted items using natural materials by local artist would be appropriate for the shop.

When purchasing merchandise to sell in the shop, you must stay in tune with your customer's likes and dislikes, their needs and desires. The hardest thing to avoid is incorporating your own personal preferences. The biggest mistake you can make is to buy merchandise based on your personal taste. You must think only in terms of your customer!

One of the most difficult challenges you will face, as a buyer, is to stop seeing the merchandise purchased through your eyes and to start viewing it through the eyes of the customer. Buying is about fulfilling the wants and needs of your customer. Your personal likes or dislikes are irrelevant. The only thing that counts is what the customer likes. And to make this challenge even more difficult, your customer's need and wants are constantly changing.

Now that you are viewing things as your customer, think of what merchandise you would expect in this type of gift shop located in this type of setting. For example, a museum gift shop exhibiting works by modern artists may want to stock gift cards by those same artists or books on the subject matter. Hospital gift shops should have all the basics: gum, toothpaste, and books, but also stock gifts for newborns or gift baskets and fresh flowers for patients.

Now you have a list of the merchandise, applicable to your shop.......
Souvenirs, collectibles, art objects, gift items, drugs & sundries, greeting
cards, magazines, books, other paper products, jewelry, candy, other food
items, plush, dolls, toys, baby items, clothing. Combine these different
types of items into departments. Souvenirs, collectable and gifts could be
a department called GIFTS. Plush, dolls, toys could be TOYS. Group like
items until you have four or five different departments. Now solicit or
appoint a buyer for each department.

STARTING OUT

When you have a buyer for each shop department, you will automatically
have a buying committee. This committee should form guide lines for
making purchases. The committee should list the duties and requirements
for this responsibility. Buying isn't just pointing to a picture in a catalogue,
or running to the market place and grabbing whatever item strikes your
fancy. Besides time and energy, it takes market research. Here's a
suggested list of the overall duties and requirements for each buyer:

DUTIES OF THE BUYER:

- ✓ The buyer should participate in all of the shop's workshops and
  sales meetings.
- ✓ The buyer should make their own appointments with vendors
  and salespersons.
- ✓ The buyer should take part in making the yearly budget for the
  shop.
- ✓ The buyer should do market research by visiting other gift
  shops, etc. and be aware of what is selling.
- ✓ The buyer should be available to check, unpack, and price all
  merchandise ordered in their department.

REQUIREMENTS:

- ✓ The buyers must work as regular attendants in the shop.
- ✓ The buyers must take part in establishing buyer's policies, so they will understand what is expected of them. (Buyers policy suggestion is in the manual.) A policy regarding the buyers is essential.
- ✓ The buyer should be involved in targeting the customer.
- ✓ The buyer should be able to attend at least one market trip per year and take part in required seminar/workshops.
- ✓ The buyer must observe the policy on making personal purchases at the markets.
- ✓ The buyer should buy within the limits of the gift shop budget.
- ✓ The buyers should understand that this is a responsible undertaking and that the success of the shop depends on their decisions.

Each buyer should be given a six month trial period to see if the items they've purchased are selling. At the end of the period the buyer and his purchasing record should be reviewed. If the merchandise purchased by a buyer is not selling, don't give up on the buyer. Instead review the guidelines with the buyer and try to find the cause and have the buyer make the necessary corrections. All buyers need to be reviewed periodically.

BUYERS BUYING

Any time the buyer will make purchases for the shop, be it on a buying trip, at a local warehouse, from a salesman/vendor or in a retail store, they should have available a list of credit references, a business card, and a pamphlet or some form of information about your organization complete with the shop's tax identification number. This information will help insure instant credit. If a company will not extend credit when provided with this information, I would recommend you not do business with them.

> **NOTE**: It is not a good idea for a buyer to give a personal credit card number to a company when establishing a new account.

Buyers should use their negotiating skill to get better credit terms for the shop, or a better price on quantity ordered. To do this you might contact the accounting department of a company and request that a percentage of the total be deducted if paid within 15 days instead of 30. You could also instruct your buyers to ask for a discount if the merchandise can be picked up (if local) instead of being delivered. Also suggest to your buyers to ask for a discount when ordering a large quantity of the same item. Or request that the company pay the freight (most do) or offer to at least split the freight charges.

Inform the buyers to ask if the vendor or manufacturer has "close out" or discontinued items that may be offered for sale at a deep discounted price. But, make sure the buyers check the merchandise first to ensure the items are salable.

Remember that in business just about everything is negotiable and it doesn't hurt to ask for a better deal - reinforce that point with your buyers. Encourage them continually to search for new suppliers and merchandise at lower prices. This is all a part of being a buyer.

THE DETAILS OF BUYING

As I've noted previously in the requirements and duties of buyers, the buyers are required to do more than just buy. They are required to check for shortages, return merchandise, and check for damages. These are all cost control measures that keep profit up and losses down. It is imperative that the buyers keep impeccable records of all purchases since many people will be involved in the handling of the merchandise. Let me walk you through the roles of a buyer, identifying where trouble spots may lie.

Let's start with the purchase order. This order should be created when the merchandise is purchased. The purchase order should be kept on file until the merchandise is received. Then when the merchandise is received there should be a packing slip in the box. This packing slip is used to check in the merchandise and should be kept until the invoice is received from the company where you purchased the merchandise. The merchandise should be marked with the retail price. Also, at the time the merchandise is received the buyer should check for damages and shortages. The company needs to be notified immediately of the damages and shortages. It is the buyer's responsibility to do so.

The individual buyer who placed the order should be responsible for checking in and pricing the items, since they will be dealing with the supplier's sales person or customer service if there is damage or shortages. That way, they will have first hand information about the condition of the order. Only the buyer knows what they have purchased, so it makes sense for them to be responsible for checking in the merchandise.

If the buyer is not available when the merchandise is received, they should leave the purchase order along with any information regarding the shipment and the retail price of each item, and request that a shop attendant price the merchandise for sale in the shop. The buyer should leave explicit instructions for handling order discrepancies for the shop attendant.

After the merchandise is checked in, priced and on the shelves, the manager or buyer submits the invoices to be paid to an accounting manager or the organization's treasurer (the person that pays the bills). Three copies of the invoice should be made - one for the shop, one for the buyer, and one for the person paying the bills. (It is a good idea for the buyer to keep the original purchase order, packing slip and a copy of the invoice in their file.) The person paying the bills gets the original invoice and the copy to send to the company along with the payment. It is a good idea to send a copy of the invoice along with the payment. This will prevent any mix-ups, which could and do occur and will eliminate a lot of headaches.

It would be a good practice for the person paying the bills, to make a copy of the original invoice that indicates payment total, check number and date paid to give to the shop manager to file in the shop. This way the manager will have a reference if a question arises about the payment of a bill.

What happens if something has to be returned because it's damaged, defective or missing? The buyer should notify the supplier immediately of any discrepancy. Keep a copy of the invoice at hand during the contact for invoice and item numbers. Make sure the buyer explains what is damaged or defective, or the number of items shorted and ask how they want to handle the problem. The manufacturer or supplying company should pay the freight or postage for returns. Most companies will issue a "call tag" for returns if the merchandise is shipped by UPS. The buyer should write this number down on the invoice and let the shop attendant know that UPS will be coming by to pick up the item.

From there, typically the manufacturer will contact UPS and the UPS driver will receive an order to pick up the merchandise to be returned and issue a receipt, which should be filed along with a copy of the invoice. It is important to save this receipt, as it is your only proof that the merchandise was picked up by UPS. The buyer should have the merchandise boxed and ready for the return. Your account will be credited after the return is received.

If the company requests that you return the items by mail (USPS), always insure the merchandise and document what is being returned. It is a good idea to get USPS delivery confirmation. The amount of postage for the return should be deducted from the invoice. If there is a shortage inform the company that the amount will be deducted from the invoice.

> **NOTE**: *Returning damaged and defective item is an effective cost control.*

If you don't want to task each buyer with returns, you could have one person in charge of returning merchandise. But I have found that it works better if the individual buyer deals with the company since they are the ones who have the contacts and have first hand knowledge of the items.

INVENTORY SOURCES

Inventory is the merchandise sitting on the shelves, in the storeroom, and on the displays ready to be purchased. Inventory, also includes supplies you use to create and assemble items to sell, and the supplies used in the running of the business. If you make gifts to sell in the shop, all the materials that go into assembling the product is considered inventory. So where do you start when you need to purchase?

There are many different sources where you can buy the merchandise that will turn into your inventory. Let me give you a quick rundown of the options. You can purchase merchandise at wholesale cost from manufacturers through major markets, catalogs, sales representatives, and vendors representing manufacturers. You can also order from many of these suppliers over the Internet. Most major companies have a web site and provide an online catalog for you to place orders.

You can also purchase merchandise at craft markets and from an individuals selling arts and crafts work. Merchandise can be purchased for resale from department stores close-out sales or discount or wholesale outlets. The volunteers in the organization can create and craft items to sell in the shop. The shop could even accept donations of used merchandise for resale.

One shop manager I know solicited donation of jewelry from the volunteers. The donated items were sorted, the silver pieces cleaned, the earrings were sterilized and then the items were put on cards for resale. This idea proved to be a good money maker and was a source of 'pure profit'. I also know, of a hospital shop manager that struck up a friendship with a manager of a large franchised retail card shop. That card shop manager donated dated, but salable merchandise to the hospital gift shop. The gift shop volunteers dusted off the donated merchandise and resold it in the shop for a 100% profit.

The inventory represents the money invested to obtain profit goals you've set. Buying and selling depends on good inventory management. It is a balancing act between keeping enough inventory on hand so a sale is not lost, while keeping the investment in inventory as low as possible. The balancing act also requires keeping as many different items on hand as necessary, while maintaining a large quantity of your fastest moving items. Selective volume buying is also a part of inventory management and to purchase the right products you need to know the right places to go. In the following sections I'll give you some general overviews of where the best places to find inventory for your shop's needs are.

TO MARKET! TO MARKET!

No where else can you learn so much about retailing and merchandising than at "market". Every type of product available for sale can be viewed and purchased for resale at these major markets located in major metropolitan areas. Most large cities will have a market center or local shows for the purchase of wholesale gift items. St. Louis, Kansas City, Baltimore, Portland, Columbus, Las Vegas, Orlando to name a few. Boston has a yearly show that is excellent for museum shops.

Each of these major market centers have thousands of showrooms occupying million of square feet, filled with zillions of products. This is, by far, the best way to purchase your merchandise. You are able to physically see and touch products that you could resell in your shop. You are able to compare, reject, select and purchase what you need all in one place. Also major markets introduce new products and trends, exposing you to new merchandising techniques and ideas which mean you have a jump on your competition.

Listed below are the five **major markets** in the United States:

Atlanta	800-ATL-MART	www.americasmarket.com
Chicago	800-677-6278	www.mmart.com
Dallas	800-DAL-MKTS	www.dallasmarketcenter.com
Los Angeles	800-LAMART4	www.lamart.com
New York	800-272-SHOW	www.nygiftfair.com

I recommend if you live within driving distance to explore these markets.

But you will have to do some planning before you get in the car or hop a plane and head out for the major market city nearest you.

Planning the trip

First you will need to register for the market you will attend. This can be done by phone or on the Market's web site.

If this initial contact is by phone, request a registration form and a listing of gift market dates and times. Tell them about your organization, so that included in the registration packet will be information on special seminars or programs that may be of specific interest to your buyers. You can, also, register on the web site of the market you plan to attend. These different sites list dates of all types of markets and provide a lot of pertinent information. By phone or online, I recommend that you visit the web site. The sites will have a map of the market and a listing all vendors. This will help in the planning.

The Dallas Market Center site has all the information that a buyer needs to know when attending a market in Dallas. Their market suggestions would be helpful for any market trip anywhere.

From there, if you have not had the opportunity to visit a market before, try to find someone that has and take them on your buying trip or at least have them participate in planning a schedule to be followed while at market. If you really want to make the most of the buying trip, at market, you must have a schedule listing the different showrooms you want to visit and the merchandise you would like to purchase because there are just too many things to see and do in a single visit. If you don't plan properly, you will be like "a kid in a candy shop", not knowing which way to turn or what 'goodie' to buy. You must make a list of what you intend to accomplish while at the market, but do save some time for exploration.

Make lodging reservations well in advance of the market dates, as most hotels or motels near market fill up fast during these shows. Most places provide free transportation to and from the market center

The volunteer organization should decide on the number of buying trips to a major market, per year. The organization should pay for the transportation, lodging and seminar cost on the buying trips, requesting that the buyers pay for their meals. All costs, other than personal purchases, paid for by the individual during these buying trips can be taken off their income tax as a charitable donation.

What should you bring?

Being prepared can make the difference between a successful experience and a frustrating one. Here is a checklist of the absolute musts to bring along:

- ✓ An estimate of how much you plan to spend
- ✓ Purchase plan by categories or showrooms
- ✓ Business cards to leave with vendors and other contacts (f you do not have business cards now would be a good time to have a few printed up with a space provided for each buyer to write in their name and contact information)
- ✓ Brochure about the institution/facility that you represent
- ✓ Credit information including your bank and financial resources and re-sale license or local sales tax ID number (Many buyers create a simple sheet with all their pertinent information to give to vendors. If you do so, bring multiple copies)
- ✓ A schedule for preferred merchandise delivery dates and cancellation dates
- ✓ Calculator
- ✓ Note pad and pen
- ✓ **Comfortable Shoes!!!**
- ✓ A bottle of aspirin and some chewable antacids.

What should you buy?

Deciding what to buy at Market is be one of the most complicated parts of running a gift shop. But at the same time the most enjoyable. A successful market experience results in just one thing--stocking your shelves. To do that, you have to shop smart and buy aggressively. Here's a list of suggestion on how to do just that:

✓ Review your inventory to see what you already have so you can avoid duplication and over-buying.

✓ Take a long look at the budget and know how much you have to spend for each classification of merchandise you will purchase at market.

✓ When buying always think in terms of retail value. Once products are in your store, it doesn't matter how much you paid for an item, only how much you can get for it.

✓ Come to Market not only to review products and trends, but also to write orders…to ensure you get the earliest access to the latest merchandise.

✓ Review freight charges to be added to your order and factor these expenses in to understand the full cost of your order.

✓ Write orders in the showroom or booth.

✓ Always include a shipping date and a cancellation date on any order placed. Ask about the shipping method and when the order might arrive.

✓ Always keep copies of all orders to track and confirm charges.

✓ COD orders aren't recommended. Use a credit card if you haven't established a credit history with a particular vendor.

✓ Follow this steadfast rule: **Buy What Sells.** Your personal likes or dislikes are irrelevant. The only thing that counts is what the customer likes, that's what sells!

While at Market you will want to build a rapport with the vendors or manufacturers, you feel you will be doing the most business with doing the coming year. Here are some tips on how to build a respected relationship with them while at Market:

- Remember that you are the **purchasing agent for your customer and not the selling agent for the manufacturer**. Keep your customer in mind.
- From the very beginning, build your relationships with vendors on honorable, ethical and respectful terms.
- Remember that manufacturers are entitled to a profit - just as you are - and that any attempts to "chisel" pricing shows the vendor you're attempting to obtain more than you are due to receive.
- Respect that vendors have the right to sell to other retailers and understand the legal obligations of the buyer in any deal.
- Price is only one factor in the final decision to buy. Take time to learn the vendor's pricing philosophy and always keep quality in mind.
- Set a quality standard for your vendors: Are they reliable? Is the product in demand? Is the pricing realistic? How is the service?
- Nurture your vendor relationships, and as they evolve, explore the availability of special discounts or incentives with your vendors.
- Demonstrate your reliability as a regular buyer who handles payment promptly and abides by agreements.

Terms used in buying:

Knowledge of these terms are crucial to communicating business transactions at Market, as well as when doing the ordering from the shop. Some of these terms have already been defined in previous chapters but since these are basic terms specifically used at Market, I have listed them here to simplify your buying experience and make it more enjoyable.

At once: term used to have merchandise shipped immediately

A.S.A.P.: term used to have merchandise shipped as soon as possible

Billing address: address where merchandise invoice is to be sent

Bill of lading: document for shipments as evidence of carrier's receipt of the shipment and as a contract between carrier and shipper

Back order: merchandise not shipped with initial order - will be shipped at a later date

Cancellation date: the date beyond which order will not be accepted (extremely important to include this date on order)

C.O.D.: cash on delivery - simply means that merchandise must be paid for when it arrives in store

Close-out: merchandise offered at a reduced price to clear out existing vendor inventory

Consignment: merchandise shipped to a retailer with the understanding that the ownership of merchandise remains with vendor until merchandise is sold

Dating: the practice of allowing retailer to pay for merchandise at a later than normal due date - always inquire if dating is available

F.O.B.: freight on board - indicates the location the merchandise was shipped from (FOB factory means retailer will pay for freight from factory - FOB Atlanta means vendor will pay freight to Atlanta)

Freight allowance: allowances given to retailer to cover all or part of freight cost

Guaranteed sale: an agreement whereby a buyer can return unsold goods after they have been exposed for sale for given period; important to get in writing

H.F.C.: hold for confirmation - simply means that order is placed but must have Shop's confirmation before it is shipped

Keystone: getting a 50% mark-up on merchandise purchased and priced at retail; it also means doubling the cost of the merchandise to obtain a retail price

Mark-up: the amount added to cost to determine the retail of item (i.e. an item that has a cost of $5 and is marked to $10 equals a 50 percent mark-up - an item that has a cost of $4 and is marked to $10 equals a 60 percent mark-up); mark-up is always calculated off retail

Markdown: to lower the price of an item for whatever reason; the amount used is always taken from retail and reduced accordingly

O.H.: this is used as an abbreviation for stock "on hand"

O.O.: this is a term used as an abbreviation for merchandise "on order"

Open-to-buy: a term used to inform a buyer of amount of dollars that are available for a given period

P.O.: this is an abbreviation for "purchase order," which is the document that instructs the vendor to ship merchandise

R.T.V.: a term used to describe any merchandise that is being "returned to vendor"

Ship date: date that merchandise is to be shipped

Ship to: address where merchandise will be shipped

Terms: the combination of the length of time to pay invoice as well as any discounts that may be arranged

Turnover: a term used to describe the number of times merchandise is bought and sold during the year; it is calculated by dividing the average inventory into the annual sales

Never buy an item on first impulse. Take time to consider the big picture. You may want to pack a small camera, to record and help you remember what you purchased or what you might want to order a later date.
Have fun!

BUYING BY CATALOG

If the buyers are unable to attend a market before your shop's opening, then start lining up suppliers to order the merchandise inventory and business supplies to get started. Some small volunteer operated shops order all their merchandise from catalogs or by placing orders with salespersons.

If you haven't been in contact with other non-profit gift shops, now is the time to make contact. They are eager to share their experiences with you, as they in turn learn from you. I know of a paid hospital gift shop manager and a volunteer manager of another hospital shop that organized a group of hospital gift shop managers in a large metropolitan area. They now have over a dozen members from different hospitals in the area. The group meets every six months to share their experiences and their lists of suppliers and wholesalers. During the rest of the year they contact each other by fax and phone for new suppliers and support. Remember, two heads are always better than one, and what you miss others may pick up on.

Visit with a retail for-profit gift shop manager, in you area. Most shop owners have had years of valuable experience and are, also, glad to share their knowledge. They have the latest information on merchandise and usually know the best companies to deal with when purchasing merchandise through a catalog. Also check the yellow pages of the phone book under "gifts wholesale".

Now, that you have a list of sources for merchandise. Call the companies and request catalogs. Credit applications and order forms are usually inserted in the catalog.

Purchasing merchandise from a catalog is not an easy task, especially if you are not familiar with the merchandise. Be aware that catalog photos and illustrations may flatter the products and may make items appear larger than actual size, so pay attention to the description of the item, noting dimensions, colors, etc. Study the catalog carefully. When first starting out with catalog buying, place the minimum order especially if the company is new or offers merchandise from an unknown manufacturer. Also remember that some companies have catalogs on the Internet and you can shop right on line.

To help you get started below is a list of suppliers that cater to non-profit shops. I've used all of these companies and have had good success with them. Just call the 800 number and ask for their catalog.

✓ **Berkeley Designs**
(800) 272-3872
✓ **EJ Enterprises**
(800) 279-8065
✓ **Mike Feinberg**
(800) 245-1689
✓ **Mayer's Giftware**
(800) 952-5667
✓ **Russ Berrie & Company, Inc.**
(800) 358-8278 Petaluma, California
(800) 272-7877 Cranbury, New Jersey

After you have made a few calls requesting catalogs, it won't be long before salespersons and vendors are knocking at your door. So, now, let's talk about buying through sales reps.

BUYING THROUGH SALES REPS & VENDORS

Sales representatives (sales reps, sales executives, account executives, vendors or whatever they call themselves) can, and oftentimes do represent one or more companies or manufacturers. Until you have established a rapport with the sales person and until they have gotten to know your shop, trust your own instincts on buying. Don't let them sway you with sales incentives or gimmicks. Because sales people can be so persuasive, here are some ideas on how to stand your ground and get the right merchandise for your shop.

- Ask that a catalog be sent prior to a sales call so you can get an idea of the merchandise offered.
- Make sure you've studied the catalog and have an idea of the items you want to discuss with the sales person.
- Most importantly, the sales call should not be conducted in the shop during business hours, as it detracts from the daily operations and is detraction for the buyer.

Instead make an appointment with the salesperson before or after the shop hours. You will want the salesperson to see your shop. That way he can view the merchandise already in the shop, but not disrupt your normal business activities. Once the salesperson has an idea of what type of merchandise you carry, he or she should be able to suggest what items he carries that would be right for your shop.

Some sales reps only sell from a master catalog, with a few samples, and do not provide the shop with a catalog. It is almost impossible for the inexperienced buyer to make snap judgments on selections of merchandise to purchase, so if you run into this situation, politely tell the salesman that you do not make hasty decisions and request he leave a catalog or pamphlet with product information.

Or ask if his company has a website that displays the items electronically. Remember not all sales people are working for you; they are working for themselves and their company. That means the salesperson may not always have the shop's best interest at heart and may be trying to unload merchandise that is not salable.

Also remember that if a salesperson says this is a "one time offer" or "one of a kind deal" that the merchandise is probably not worth the offer. High-pressure tactics often signal low-volume selling items. Don't be swayed by typical salesmen tactics of flattery, bribery or coercion.

BUYING FROM CRAFT SHOWS

Since you have a team of buyers, use them! Have your buyers take a day and visit a local craft shows searching for merchandise suitable for the shop. You can never tell when you will find a bestseller at one of these shows.

In a municipal garden in Oklahoma, there's a lake called Swan Lake. In their garden gift shop, they sell a personalized ceramic swan. Where did the buyers of this shop find such a perfect item for their shop? At a craft show of all places. The manager of the shop met a lady at the show that did exquisite porcelain figurines. They started talking about the shop and the items to sell and between the two of them they came up with the perfect swan figurine customized just for the shop. And now it's their best seller! So don't overlook the most mundane opportunities to find the most unique products. Do what that manager did - look for items that can be made into exclusive gems for your shop.

> **REMEMBER:** Handmade jewelry is another item that proves to be a good purchase at a craft show. But be selective and do not over buy when dealing with any craft item.

OUTLETS AND CLOSEOUT SALES

Buying at outlets and closeout sales is another way of purchasing that requires an experienced and savvy shopper with an eye for quality merchandise, knowledge of market prices, and the stamina and time involved to rummage through merchandise in undesirable locations. But it is well worth the effort because you can find incredible deals way below cost, if you're just willing to look.

For example, many card buyers of volunteer shops go to the local card outlet or discounters to purchase greeting cards and that's where they find their highest profit making item – the greeting card. Typically, you can select cards for your type of shop or customer, and you can purchase cards individually. This is great for small shops because if you purchase through a distributor you will be required to purchase large quantities of the same design.

Once you make your purchase at one of these card outlets, you would then sell the cards in your shop at the pre-marked retail price. You make a nice profit since most of the time you'll be purchasing them at outlet shops for half price or less than cost. Also check out card and gift shops going out of business. They oftentimes offer great deals on whole sections of cards and the display racks.

But the deals don't stop at greeting cards. Some gift item manufacturers get rid of seconds or overstocked items at similar outlets. And in some instances, the merchandise is priced lower than wholesale cost. Be careful when shopping - look carefully for damage. Select items with the packaging intact.

While I'm on the topic of discount outlets, another type of discount wholesaler you should visit is Sam's or Costco. It would be a good idea to get a business account with one of these warehouse clubs in your area. They provide an array of items at wholesale prices, (including office supplies). You can also purchase candy/gum and fresh flowers for resale in the shop at these local wholesale clubs. First of all, it makes sense to purchase perishables items locally and second, they are usually priced the same as from a distributor.

Disposable cameras can be purchased at a deep discount at these clubs and these are great impulse buys especially in hospital gift shops where an expectant father might have forgotten his camera. Also such items as batteries, digital cameras, phone cards, bottled water, etc. are great items for those shops that cater to the tourist-type customer.

Most wholesale memberships run from $30-100 for business members. You should ask if they offer discounts to non-profits. In certain regions of the country, some do. Also many of these shops offer monthly billing/ charge accounts so if you needed to send a volunteer in to do the shopping they don't have to make the purchases with their own money and then get reimbursed. Plus some shops also offer up to 2% back on all purchases made through-out the year, and they oftentimes will highlight your business in their monthly newsletter for free.

BUYING FROM AN INDIVIDUAL OR SMALL COMPANY

Local artists or crafts person are always looking for outlets to display and sell their merchandise and they may call on your shop. But be selective in what you purchase so you can maintain quality in the shop. You don't want the shop to end up looking like a craft sale.

Let the artists know you seek only quality material. While you could purchase the merchandise out right, you could also put merchandise on display in the shop on a consignment basis. (Discussion of the pros and cons of consignment is in the next section.)

BUYING ON CONSIGNMENT

What does consignment mean? It means the merchandise is displayed in the shop and the supplier is paid only when the merchandise is sold. This might be a good idea for those small shops starting out to stock their shelves. But impeccable records must be kept when buying consignment merchandise. And it means you must have a workable way to tag the merchandise so that it can be identified at the time of sale and recorded for payment to the consignor. Consignment benefits both the artist/craftsman and the shop. It gives the artist a place to display their works while not tying up monies the shop has budgeted for other purchases.

It may be the just the thing for a small shop starting out with a low budget. A wide variety of selected art, crafts and handmade items taken on consignment can make the shop very unique. But I can't stress enough that consignment means more paperwork, and more potential for problems. And it's certainly not advisable to accept merchandise from more than four consignors, at a time because it just gets too confusing. If you decide consignment is right for your shop, it is advisable to have a "consignment committee" to decide on what consignment items the shop will accept.

The taste and judgment of three or four different individuals on a "consignment committee" is somewhat of an assurance that the shop will not accept inferior merchandise or merchandise catering to only one person's taste. The shop can get a variety of quality art, appealing to a wide variety of customers. Plus, the decision of accepting merchandise lies with a committee and the unpleasant task of rejecting merchandise is not the responsibility of only one person.

Typically, the committee will negotiate the percentage of the selling price of a consignment item. This committee will also assume the bookkeeping duties, making sure that the consignors understand the consignment contract and that all items listed on the contract are at the selling price, indicating the percentage of what the consignor receives and what the consignee retains. You can find an example consignment contract in *Appendix A – Business Forms*.

The committee will also educate the gift shop sales staff on how to record the consignment sale. This is very important! With a number of volunteers working in the shop, there is more room for error and more potential that a consignment item sold doesn't get properly recorded. So make sure you drill your volunteers on how to recognize and sell the consignment items. Stress to them the importance, that although you're making money for the shop by selling such items, you are also helping a (typically struggling) local artist make a few dollars as well. And it is important that the right person get the money for the consignment merchandise sold.

At the end of each month the committee takes an inventory of the consignment merchandise and records what each consignor has sold, calculates their percentage of the sales price and record what merchandise the shop has retained.

They submit the invoices to the gift shop manager or accountant for payment. The consignor is then sent a check for the percentage of merchandise sold. As you can see, selling consignment items takes a lot of extra work and bookkeeping. You really have to weigh the pros and cons carefully before deciding if this method of obtaining merchandise is right for your shop.

CONTRACT TO PURCHASE

When dealing with wholesalers, the companies provide purchase orders and invoices that serve as a contract for purchase of merchandise. But, in the course of your operations you may find it necessary to enter into an agreement with a vendor, small business, or individual that does not have a printed contract or agreement form. For example, your shop wants to sell fresh flower arrangements but you don't have the expertise to do the arranging. So you contract with a local floral shop to do the arranging, and in return for selling their merchandise/service, you give them a percentage of the sale. Since the shop has a captive customer ready to buy, it's an easy sale for the florist and is good advertising to boot, while at the same time accommodating both the customer and the shop.

To set up such an arrangement, you will need a contract so that both the shop and the small company knows exactly what is expected of each party. The easiest way to come up with an agreement is to list what you expect from the person providing the merchandise and what you will do to compensate for the sale of the merchandise. Never work off just a verbal agreement, as it's too easy for miscommunication to happen. Since it really isn't necessary (or cost effective) for the volunteer shop to hire a lawyer, draw up a simple contract yourself. For examples of such simple contracts, visit Nolo Press (www.nolopress.com) or check out several of their books on small business contracts. A sample contract, labeled "Vendor Contract" used for business between a hospital and florist can be found in Appendix A- Business Forms.

When people representing businesses enter into an agreement, but neglect to put it in writing, there may be a misunderstanding later. It is imperative to put in writing, in contract form, any transactions that involve money. It forces both parties to be specific in their agreement. It protects both parties and provides a point of reference when a question arises. In the contract each party promises to do something for the other party in exchange for a product or compensation. Organizations, businesses or institutions or facilities that have volunteer organization/auxiliaries have in-house counsel and it is advisable to have their lawyers look over the contract before it is presented to the other party.

> **NOTE**: *Sample contracts for consignments, contract for accepting merchandise from small businesses, contract for purchasing merchandise from an individual or small business and blank purchase order form are found in Appendix A- Business Forms.*

It is rare, but you might find that a company or supplier that you are ordering from does not provide a purchase order form or you might be doing business with an individual and you will need a record of what has been ordered.

The following is a sample purchase order, and a blank form can be found in *Appendix A – Business Forms.*

PURCHASE ORDER EXAMPLE:

Here's an example of a purchase order listing a variety of items typically purchased in a hospital gift shop.

PURCHASE ORDER

ORDER # 1205

DATE: 1/1/2006

**A CANDY COMPANY
ORDER CITY, USA**

PHONE: 1-800-811-0000

ITEM #	DESCRIPTION	QUANITY	UNIT COST	EXTENSION	RETAIL
5402	IT'S A GIRL CANDY BALLOON 9"	6	2.75	16.50	5.99
5403	IT'S A BOY CANDY BALLOON 9"	6	2.75	16.50	5.99
4302	GET WELL CANDY BALLOON/L SUGFREE	6	3.00	18.00	6.50
4303	GET WELL CANDY BALLOON/L HARD CANDY	6	2.75	16.50	5.99
3101	CHOCOLATE CIGARS BOY	12 boxes	4.25	51.00	9.50
3102	CANDY CANE BOY CIGARS	12 boxes	3.25	39.00	6.99
3300	BUBBLE GUM GIRL CIGARS	12 boxes	6.75	81.00	13.99
	TOTAL				$238.50

The purchase order is necessary for a shop where persons other then the buyer may be receiving merchandise. The buyer doing the ordering should file or post the purchase order in the shop so that when the merchandise comes in it can be checked against the packing slip or invoice. This ensures there is no mistake about what was ordered. The retail price should be included on the purchase order.

Note to museum shops: Buying for the museum shop is different. You can useall the suggestions on purchasing listed above but as you may already know There is an organization dedicated to this type of merchandise, the Museum Store Association. There are approximately 1,800 museums in the United States that belong to the Museum Store Association, all of which either have a store or are in the process of opening this type of retail operation.

Founded in 1955, the MSA is an international organization representing museum store professionals worldwide. MSA is a nonprofit organization dedicated to the general welfare of the museum store industry, and it helps museum store managers better serve their institutions and the public. MSA member stores range in net sales from less than $5,000 to more than $17 million. Museum stores sell items that provide visitors with souvenirs and educational materials directly related to their museum experience. You can learn more about MSA by visiting their website at (http://www.museumdistrict.com).

The title of this chapter, "Purchasing Ins and Outs" says it all. That is just what should be happening; the purchases should come in and go right out. If this is not occurring in your shop, you need to review the buying methods. Get in the habit of taking a physical inventory monthly to see what items are moving from the shelves and what is still there. Have the gift shop volunteers make note of customer requests.

We have investigated the various ways to purchase merchandise for the shop. We have established that we are purchasing for the customer. We have to know the ins and outs of all the various methods. You can see that the buyers have an important job. The success of the shop depends on the right purchasing decisions. If the merchandise purchased does not sell, then you will not have sales. Next, to arrive at the right price for this merchandise let's discuss pricing, and then see how various factors influence sales.

PRICING

Last but not least, we have to talk about pricing. I personally feel that fair pricing is the best policy. Most of the volunteer shops when pricing gift items use the method of "keystoning". This is just a term for doubling the cost of the item including shipping costs. Another good policy is to price high enough to cover what costs you incur and low enough to build sales volume. The main thing to remember when pricing is that the price is 'what the customer is willing to pay'.

> *REMEMBER: Don't forget to include the cost of shipping. You will want to consider shipping costs when arriving at a retail price.*

Here are a few formulas I've used for coming up with the right pricing for items purchased. The most simplistic formula is again this one:

Mark-up of at least 100% - SIMPLY DOUBLE THE COST

The following more extensive formulas are used in non-profit gift shops and are suggested for a higher profit. These formulas usually price items less than regular retail shops. Remember you don't want to get a reputation for gouging your customers, so use these formulas as a guide. And also remember, since the overhead is considerably lower in this type of shop, the mark-up on merchandise can be lower.

Pricing Formulas:

Gifts, Toys, Plush: **Cost x 2.1**
Jewelry: **Cost x 2.5**
Sundries: **Cost x 1.5 to Cost x 2 or suggested retail**
Greeting Cards: **Suggested retail**

Occasionally items can be purchased at an exceptional discount and should be priced at suggested retail or what the market will bring. This is not gouging your customer, it's really just good business.

REMEMBER: YOU LOSE MONEY ON ANY ITEM THAT IS REDUCED BY 50% OR MORE!

While it is necessary to have formulas, methods and guidelines for pricing, creative pricing should not be ruled out. Know your customer, what they are willing to pay and know the market. Visit other shops and do some comparative shopping on prices. This is necessary. Now if you have an item that cannot be purchased anywhere else but in your shop or you have an item that is in high demand, use creative pricing. Pricing at what the market will bring.

Chapter 10

Tenth Step: Get Up and Running!

The shop is completed, the fixtures are installed, the paperwork is done, the merchandise is on the shelves, the necessary equipment for doing business is in place and the volunteers are trained. Now you're ready for the <u>GRAND OPENING!</u>

GRAND OPENING

A grand opening (or re-opening) is one of the best ways to attract attention to your shop. A grand opening can last a single night, a week or a month. Start with a grand opening party. Make a list of potential 'movers and shakers' in your area and perspective or former customers. Include the employees of the institution or facility and the volunteers of your organization in your list. Then print invitations and mail or deliver them to these community members.

If you're on a tight budget, for a nominal cost the invitations can be made on the computer. An example is shown below. You could either print up a number of copies from the computer on white or colored card stock purchased at an office supply shop, or you could take your master copy and have your local copy shop print them. I've saved money by making four invitations on a single 8½ x 11 sheet, and cut them into cards with a paper cutter (4 ¼ x 5 ½). I then stuffed the invitations into 4 ⅜ x 5 ¾ envelopes that can, also, be purchased at your local office supply shop. Such inexpensive tasteful invitations not only did the trick by getting out the pertinent information, but also signaled to the invitee that our organization was not only frugal but consciously using money wisely.

YOU ARE CORDIALLY INVITED TO THE

Hospital Gift Shop

Open House

Celebrating the Grand Opening on

Monday, March 5, 2003
6:00-9:00 p.m.

205 Hospital Road

Your Town, State

A Sample Inexpensive Invitation
Note: You can find more sample invitations you can print from your printer at
www.microsoft.com/office or **www.avery.com**.

DAY TO DAY MANAGEMENT

The shop will need a staff to handle day-to-day operations. Besides a manager, I've found that an assistant manager, a scheduling manager, a business and/or accounting manager, plus three or four buyers is the ideal staff for a small shop. You may decide to have more or less on your volunteer staff. The idea is to surround yourself with the most talented and willing workers in your organization. Undoubtedly, the job of running a business can be overwhelming so the shop will need a lot of dedicated help.

Follow Henry Ford's advice when he said "Nothing is particularly hard if you divide it into small jobs". But how, where and which activities would you delegate? Here are a few suggestions on how to divide the work and responsibilities into smaller jobs.

Here's a quick overview of the list of roles and responsibilities I'd recommend. Later I've detailed each volunteer's roles in depth.

- **Manager** – responsible for the overall operation of the shop
- **Assistant Manager** – the backup for the manager
- **Scheduling Manager** – responsible for scheduling all volunteers
- **Business / Accounting Manager** – responsible for an accounting/business practices
- **Buyers** - responsible for purchasing inventory sold in the shop

Now let's examine each volunteer roll in detail. For small shops this may sound like overkill. But remember, volunteers have limited time, and the one thing you don't want to do is cause burn out with your volunteers by having them take on too many responsibilities.

MANAGER

The manager is responsible for the overall operation of the gift shop. Although managers may delegate, their main roles in the shop include:

- **In the service to the organization -**
  Strives to conduct the operations of the shop in a business like manner, considers all suggestions and constructive criticism and acts as a liaison between each volunteer, the organization, administration, and the community.

- **Appoints -**
  an assistant, scheduling, and accounting manager

- **Appoints -**
  the necessary buyers and coordinate all buying

- **Holds workshops or sales meetings at least twice a year**

- **Compiles an annual budget**
  And submits an annual report to the volunteers, volunteer organization and the administration of the host organization

- **Oversees all publicity and advertising for the shop**

- **Determines a merchandise mark-up to assure profit**

- **Is responsible for all incoming merchandise -**
  check all purchase orders, invoices and statements

ASSISTANT MANAGER

The Assistant Manager not only assists the manager in all of his duties, but also learns the duties of the manager to assume that position if the need arises. More specifically, the Assistant Manager:

- Sees to the daily operations
- Conducts all inventories
- Takes over any duties the Manager is unable to perform

ACCOUNTING MANAGER

The Accounting Manager handles all the financial aspects of the shop including:

- Paying all bills
- Settling the daily receipts
- Making all the bank deposits
- Keeping all the records of the shop
- Preparing and presenting all the financial reports

SCHEDULING MANAGER

The Scheduling Manager is responsible for the scheduling of the gift shop staff. The duties of the Scheduling Manager include:

- Scheduling staff to attend gift shop.
- Posting a monthly work schedule calendar
- Finding substitutes when necessary
- Recruiting volunteers for the shop
- Taking part in staff training

In a volunteer organization the distribution of the responsibilities and workload with 3 assistant managers is imperative. The responsibilities of the entire shop should not rest on one person.

BUYERS

Note: The duties and responsibilities of the buyers are found in Chapter 9, 'Purchasing Inventory -The Ins and Outs'.

MANNING THE SHOP
Volunteer Training

You have already started to fill slots for sales persons in the shop with the managing staff. Each person on the staff should be required to work in the shop at least one shift per week. But you will need volunteer sales persons to man the shop. To recruit volunteers for the gift shop try these tricks that have worked for me:

- Solicit your friends and neighbors
- Submit ads for volunteers in local newspapers
- Make pleas to local churches
- Post Volunteer information in the local library or community college (Most colleges and libraries have a bulletin board for community events where the plea for volunteers could be posted)

To keep good volunteers, provide the best working conditions possible. Provide the necessary equipment for making the operations of the shop convenient. Encourage the volunteer to participate in planning. Provide a suggestion box and encourage input. Let the volunteers know that their opinions are valuable. Provide a safe, convenient work place with structure and meaning. The volunteer deserves that!

You must treat all volunteers with respect by creating a professional and business-like atmosphere in the shop, by delegating responsibilities, recognizing contributions and sharing the goals and successes. Recruiting, retaining and motivating dedicated volunteers are the keys to unlocking "the doors to success" to your gift shop.

The volunteer sales staff should be trained to provide professional and caring service. The key to this training of volunteers is to give the volunteer a strong sense of purpose, to build on the volunteer strengths and minimize their weaknesses or lack of experience. Duties should be specific in details.

When a new volunteer expresses a desire to work in the shop, show them around and introducing them to other persons working there. Provide them with a shop manual and explain that all policies and procedures are listed in the manual. Go over a few of the most important ones now and as you go through the training. Let them ask questions about the merchandise. Show them where to find the price sticker on the merchandise. Tell them what to do incase the item is not priced. (all of this is in the manual, but this information is understood better if it is reiterated in the training process.) Point out the fast sellers in the shop. Give hands-on training on the cash register. Go through the steps in making a sale, from greeting the customer to sacking the merchandise. Go through the "check-out" steps in completing a sale. Show them that the answers to almost all of the questions they will have while manning the shop can be found in the manual. Show them that there is a step-by-step procedure of the operations of all machines in the shop. Show them where they can find help! Go over the building's safety procedures. Be close at hand when they wait on their first customer. A volunteer should never be left alone in the shop until they feel completely comfortable.

Remember that not all volunteers have worked in a retail setting before, so training is essential. The scheduling manager could train all volunteers instead of the manager. One person doing the training will assure consistency in the operations of the shop.

It is best to have two or more persons scheduled for each shift to insure that the shop will always be attended. This is a volunteer position, so the incentive to show up, sometimes, is not taken seriously. More than one person scheduled for each shift assures that the shop will always be open. With an additional person in the shop, there will always be someone to run errands, provide a break, or just be there just for moral support and companionship. And this is what part of volunteering is all about.

The volunteer, in order to be more productive, should be required to attend scheduled sales meetings. It would be ideally to have sales meetings each Monday morning to start of the week, as most traditional retailer do. But in the volunteer world this is not a good idea. Most volunteers do not want to spend more than one day a week at a volunteer job.

Too many meetings may drive away even your most dedicated volunteer. I have found two sales meetings per year are sufficient with one meeting per year as mandatory attendance for each volunteer. A sales meeting or workshop should be announced in advance and should be well planned. Suggestions for the meetings:

1. A safety meeting that would include personal safety in the shop, fire and disaster procedures as well as shoplifting and theft. The safety officer of the organization or a local police officer could be invited as guest speaker.
2. Review of "check-out". Cash register operation including charge, lay-a-way and employee payroll deduction would be reviewed.
3. Review of the manual and manual revision.
4. Demonstration of a handmade craft item to sell in the shop. This will start those creative juices flowing among the staff and recruit your most talented workers for projects.

The most popular and productive sales meetings are the simulations of daily operations, where those in attending, role-play different situation that occur in the shop. Acting out the process of a cash, check or credit card sale is one example of simulations. This meeting could also include problems that have been encountered in the shop in the past year and the solutions.

DAILY ROUTINE

The explanation of daily operations should include:

- The time the volunteer/employee enters the area until the time they leave at the end of their shift.
- Information on dress code, uniform, etc.
- Parking designated areas.
- Instructions on entrance to the building.
- Where to sign or clock-in.
- Step-by-step instructions for opening and closing the shop.
- Policies and procedures that will be used in daily operations.
- Instructions of machine operations should be included and suggestions for making running of the shop easier.
  These things are the part of the daily operations and are included in your operations manual. (Chapter 5)

Give the volunteer more information than they actually need in order for the daily operations to run smoothly. Information on upcoming sales and promotions should be made available to the volunteer. Post current information, vital to daily operations, on the shop's bulletin board. Another way of keeping your volunteers informed is writing a weekly newsletter and sending it via email. The customer expects assistance from the volunteer attendant operating the shop, just as they would in any other retail shop, so that is imperative that the volunteer know what is happening in the shop in order to provide good customer service.

The volunteer needs to be reminded that they are there to provide a service not only to the shop and organization, but also to the customer. The volunteer represents the shop and everything they do effects how the customer will remember their experience in the shop. This experience will become a lasting impression of the institution or organization.

The three basic steps of selling that reflects good customer service should be reviewed with each volunteer during training. These steps include:

1. The Greeting - All customers should be acknowledged when they enter the shop. Make eye contact with the customer. In the section on Shoplifting, later in this chapter, the benefit of eye contact is discussed as a no cost way to reduce shoplifting.

2. Offer to Assist - To gain information of the customers needs. This can be as simple as asking the customer the question, "How may I help you?"

3. Offer suggestion - Make suggestion that will meet the customer's needs. A non-aggressive way to make a suggestion is as simple as making a statement about an item, such as, "We just received this yesterday" or "Have you seen this new item?" And always suggest an extra item that will enhance the purchase, such as a gift bag or card.

Acquaint your volunteers about your best selling items. One of the best selling tools is product knowledge. This is especially true in the museum or zoo setting because education is the purpose of these facilities. The volunteer that is knowledgeable about the merchandise will be able to educate the customer and enhance a purchase, satisfying the customer and ultimately selling more.

You will want to convey to the volunteer the importance of keeping good records. To help the volunteer do this, a Daily Receipt Form could be used to manually record sales if you are operating out of a cash drawer or the register printout does not contain record keeping information.

It is also a good reference for the manager or buyers to review and identify items that are selling. But if you have an up to date register with inventory tracking or a POS system this would not be necessary.

A Daily Reconciliation Form for reconciling the receipts at the end of the day is needed, no matter what type of check-out system you use. This can be printed on the other side of the Daily Receipt Form and kept near the cash register.

Following are examples of each form I've used. Feel free to use and modify them as you see fit. You can also find pre-designed forms at www.microsoft.com/office/templates or at your local office supply store. At the end of this book are also example forms you can easily copy and use as you need.

DAILY RECEIPT FORM

#sold	Description	Price	%off	Sale	Tax	Total	**Total**
1	Plush animal	10.00			.65	10.65	
2	Hair clips	2.25		4.50	.29	4.79	15.44
3	Candy Bars	.50		1.50	.10	1.60	17.04
1	Gund Teddy Bear	19.99					

Total Merchandise sold at the end of the shift_____

DAILY RECONCILIATION FORM

NET SALES   1,349.00

TAX   87.69

TOTAL $1436.69

CREDIT CARD
SALES   588.88

CHECKS   252.36

CASH   595.45

(LINE 3 MINUS LINES 4 AND 5)

TOTAL $ 1436.69
(SHOULD BE THE SAME AS LINE 3)

COMMENTS:

_____

NOTE: *See Appendix A – Business Forms for forms ready to copy and use*

Suggested list of duties for daily operations:

CHECK LIST OF DUTIES FOR REGISTER ATTENDANT

_____Wipe phones handheld equipment with disinfectant wipes

_____Check supply of cash register tape

_____Check supply of credit card forms

_____Check supply of other needed forms

_____Stock all candy/gum/snacks

_____Stock sundries

_____Stock camera, film and batteries

_____Stock bags, boxes and tissue

_____Stock floral cards

_____Clean glass counter tops

CHECK LIST FOR FLOOR ATTENDANT

_____Check to see if all merchandise is priced

_____Fold or organize apparel by size and design

_____Clean flower cooler and replace water in arrangements

_____Water plants and remove wilted foliage

_____Straighten greeting cards

_____Restock paper products

_____Restock all gift items as needed

_____Straighten shelves in storeroom

SAFETY IN THE DAILY OPERATIONS

PERSONAL SAFETY

The personal safety of the volunteer is critical. There may be a misconception, that since the volunteer attendant is not paid, that they are responsible for their own safety. This is not true. The organization, host organization, municipality, company, corporation, etc. is legally responsible for the safety of the volunteers while they are on duty. This organization will have a safety officer, safety codes, rules and regulations. Each volunteer or paid attendant should be made aware of these codes, rules and regulations. A list of safety procedures should be posted in the shop. The safety procedures, codes, rules and regulations should address disasters, fire, robbery, thief, shop lifting and personal safety in regards to machinery, tools, and equipment used on the job. Safety codes and procedures should be a mandatory part of the volunteer's orientation and training.

The organizational building safety codes may not address the following procedures regarding hygiene. These should be incorporated for the safety and welfare of the volunteer in a gift shop: Hand washing, disinfecting phone and equipment. The importance of hand washing, and what I call sterilizing or sanitizing is often overlooked in a gift shop. If a few moments are taken each morning to disinfect the phone you can help stop the spread of flu and virus germs and fewer volunteers will be out on "sick leave". It is a good idea to have handy, by the register, a can of spray disinfect and a pump bottle of waterless germicidal liquid. If you have a sink in your storeroom provide a germicidal soap for hand washing.

Persons that handle money are at risk in contacting diseases. Paper currency is commonly contaminated with bacteria and this may play a role in the transmission of potentially harmful organisms. It makes sense that paper money, passed from person to person dozens of times each day, might pick up some bacteria along the way.

Those bacteria may include organisms that cause pneumonia or blood infections. Unfortunately, there are few things we can do to avoid the germs carried by money, other than using our charge cards and frequent hand washing, particularly in a hospital environment.

THEFT & SHOPLIFTING

Unfortunately thief and shoplifting go on in a volunteer operated shop as well as the retail shop in the mall. In fact, volunteer operated shops are often targeted for thief and shoplifting. The shoplifter thinks that the volunteer manning the shop is an easy target and that even if he is caught most likely the organization will not prosecute. Policies on thief should be adopted by the organization and carried out. I would recommend that the shop post a notice that shoplifters will be prosecuted.

The best way that a volunteer manning the shop can discourage and reduce shoplifting is to greet each customer with eye contact. Persons contemplating shoplifting who know that they have been seen are less likely to commit the crime, for fear of being identified.

The volunteer should be instructed on the proper way to handle a shoplifter. For safety of the volunteer and the liability of the organization they should never approach the shoplifter or accuse them in the shop. The volunteer should actually witness the shoplifting/theft and then call security to apprehend the shoplifter outside the shop. In an alert, fully staffed shop, placement of the shop's fixtures and securing expensive items will deter shoplifting.

One day, while talking with a local Wal-Mart manager about the shoplifting problem, he gave me a copy of this sign that is posted in their shops. In *Appendix A - Business Forms*, the sign is ready for you to copy and post in your shop.

ROBBERY

Robbery of cash is not really a big problem in this type of shop, but in today's world it is a possibility and should be addressed. As with shoplifting and theft of merchandise, the more persons manning the shop, the less likely it is to occur. The difficulty for the robber to make a get-a-way and the activity in the buildings of these types of organizations usually deters a robbery.

Things to prevent robbery:

- Keep the safe out of sight.
- Do not keep large amounts of cash in the safe.
- Make daily deposits.
- Do not keep a large amount of cash in the cash drawer/register. When unfamiliar persons come into the shop requesting change for a large bill, explain that the shop does not carry a lot of cash in the register and direct them to the business or cashier office of the organization
- When the register is checked out at the end of the day, be sure the security guard is near and that there is another person on duty in the shop.
- Lock the door when the register is being checked out.
- When carrying large amounts of cash out of the building, have a security guard walk with you.
- Try not to broadcast the news when the shop has had a record day or that you are getting ready to go to the bank to make a deposit. In other words keep a low profile.
- Instruct all persons working in the shop that they should **not** to try to stop a robbery. Any amount of money is not worth an injury or loss of life.

When a robbery or shoplifting has occurred the police must be called and a police report filed. The presence of the police sends a message that shoplifting and theft will not be tolerated.

INTERNAL THEFT

Theft by volunteers or employees within a volunteer setting is another unpleasant subject that needs to be discussed. It is something we do not like to think about, but it does exist. A shop cannot survive with internal theft. The entire purpose of the organization and its roll in the community is jeopardized. It is inconceivable to think that a person volunteering their time would steal from the organization they have pledged to help. The only explanation I can come up with, is when volunteers or employees feel unappreciated and are not given respect or responsibility and are not made to feel part of the group, a theft may occur. Some people justify taking merchandise or money because they are volunteering, thinking that they are entitled, as a form of payment for their services. A paid employee in this type of shop may feel that it is not a real business and "since the money goes for charity, what difference does it make".

So, make each volunteer or employee feel that they are a vital part of the organization, that they are working together towards a common goal and this is indeed a business for the benefit of a worthy cause. It is imperative that the organization shows respect and appreciation to the volunteers. This is the greatest deterrent against internal theft. If a problem arises, alert all volunteers and ask for their assistance, without any accusations. As a last resort the manager of the shop should notify the building security and ask their assistance before starting a formal investigation. Internal theft should not be tolerated. No business can survive when merchandise, cash and supplies keep disappearing.

There are different kinds of internal thefts, you should be aware of. The theft of cash can occur when cash is stolen from the register. It may be hidden by the employee or volunteer during a sales transaction. For instance, when the sale is not rung up on the register and the payment for merchandise is pocketed or when fake refunds or voids are entered on the cash register and cash taken.

So be aware when refunds or voids are made on the register without explanation. You may need to incorporate a policy on how refunds and void are handled. Having another person in the shop 'OK' these transactions may hinder this type of internal theft.

Theft of merchandise includes not only the pocketing of merchandise by the employee or volunteer, but can be disguised when a purchase is rung up on the register at a fraction of value. Again, having two persons on duty will deter this type of theft and incorporating the policy that the volunteer or shop attendant does not record their own transactions.

Theft of supplies is rampant in every business. Keep reminding the volunteers that the costs of supplies come out of the shop's profits.

Another form of theft is the 'theft of time'. It may not seem important in a volunteer setting, but what if a volunteer does not show up or arrives late for the assigned shift, causing the shop to be robbed of lost sales. The volunteer may use time volunteered to make personal calls or do personal business. Stress that the time spent volunteering is important to the success of the shop and that, as in all other successful retail businesses, attention must be paid to business.

Other problems with in-house theft may occur with the employees of the organization outside the shop. Having the housekeeping staff of the building do the cleaning in the shop, after hours, usually presents problems. It is a good idea for the volunteers to do housekeeping chores during regular business hours. This will cut down on loss due to breakage and theft that may occur by the housekeeping staff. This will also eliminate the need for additional keys or codes for entry.

Chapter 11
Eleventh Step: Payments – Cash, Check, Charge?

Payment for purchases can be made by cash, check, or credit card. Purchases can also be made through an employee payroll deduction plan, with a lay-a-way plan, or with gift certificates. Or your gift shop may incorporate in-house charge transactions. And don't forget, people who represent an organization or businesses qualified for a tax-exempt status may make purchases in your shop. That will be a tax exempt purchase, another method of payment.

So what payment options do you want to offer your customers or will you have to offer your customer? Let's review each option. And remember, the more options you give your customers to pay, the more likely you'll have a customer who comes back time and time again.

CASH

Cash is a no-brainer and obviously one of the payment options you should offer. However, beware! Believe it or not, there are problems associated with cash. First volunteers may end up giving out the incorrect change, so having a good cash register that tells the volunteer what change to give, plus giving them a refresher course in giving correct change helps alleviate this problem. When making change, the volunteer should be trained to enter on the cash register the amount of cash tendered for payment and the register will display the correct amount in change to be given to the customer. If your register does not have this feature, the change should be counted aloud to the customer, which is not a bad idea in either case. Instructions in money handling should be included in training and the mandatory workshops. Impress on the volunteer to focus on the transaction and to not be distracted when handling money.

Another problem with cash that is growing concern is counterfeit money. But you can combat counterfeiters by utilizing some inexpensive technology. The recent introduction of redesigned $20 bills meant to thwart counterfeiters doesn't seem to be working as well as the government had hoped. So you may need to instruct the volunteer or shop attendant on the slight risk that someone would offer a counterfeit bill as payment for a purchase.

Today you can find on the market a number of devices that check for counterfeit currency. The simplest and cheapest devise is a Counterfeit Currency Detection Pen, manufactured by companies such as CIS and Keysan. Most sell for under $3 and use a special ink. How does the pen work? When you run the pen over the bill, if the ink turns dark brown or black, then the bill is suspect. Most work on money printed after 1959 and with the new currency printed after 1999. You can find them at any office supply shop. Like any pen, the ink runs out. Expect most pens to check up to 30,000 bills before replacing. A great deal!

Other, more expensive tools used in detecting counterfeit money are magnetic ink detectors, ultra violet detectors, and counterfeit money scanners. If you are in a large city, or handle large sums of money you should consider looking into one of these devices. All detection devices are easy to operate and should be used on large bills at the time of sale. If a bill turns up suspect, simply ask the customer to provide you with another bill.

CHECKS

Accepting checks takes on more risk and responsibility than cash. These days it's very easy to make counterfeit checks with a laser printer and computer. It's easy enough to make checks and even easier to steal someone's account number, and use that on the checks. So the first step in countering counterfeit checks is to make sure that all shop attendants know to take only personal, printed checks and not blank counter checks.

You could start a file of customers that will normally pay by check. Have them complete a form with pertinent information to be kept in the file. They would be issued a shop 'check cashing' number that is to be written on the check when paying for purchases. This is usually time consuming and impractical for this type of shop, but an option if you decide to accept checks for payment.

Instruct the gift shop attendant, when accepting a check they should write the drivers license number and date of birth on the front of the check, while checking to see if the picture on the license is in fact the person tendering the check. Also make sure they check that the address on the license is the same as on the check. Another important thing is to get a phone number if it is not printed on the check. Most customers are use to this routine and do not mind giving the information.

The shop attendant may also want to call the local bank that the check is written on for verification, if in doubt about the person submitting the check. Most banks these days have automated options that allow for merchants to verify checks. With these automated systems typically you supply the checking account number and the amount of the check. The bank will verify if the account can cover the amount of the check.

If the suggested safe guards are followed, and you still get more than two returned checks a month, you may need to investigate check verification systems that guarantee checks when the verification system is used. These systems utilize the check accounts, driver license numbers, and sometimes social security numbers to verify the check.

You also run the risk, when accepting a check for payment, that the funds are not available in the check writer bank account and the check is returned by the bank for non-payment.

What happens when a check is returned for non-payment? Typically the bank will return the check along with an explanation for not accepting the check. If you've done everything to verify the personal information of the check writer, it is a good idea to call the person and pleasantly explain that you have received notice than the check did not clear. Most likely by the time the bank notifies you, the customer is already aware that their check did not clear. So your call shouldn't be any big surprise to the customer, and if the customer isn't a career check bouncer, they most likely will be happy to take care of the problem immediately. When you call, state that the bank has charged you a fee for returning the check and that the shop also has a fee for returned checks, but, if they come in immediately and take care of the situation, you will waive the shop fee if they will pay the amount of the check plus the bank charge. Inform the check customer this payment must be by cash or money order and delivered to the shop within 48 hours. Nine times out of ten, the customer will be at the door the next morning with the reimbursement. Typically, gift shops charge fees of $10 and up for returned checks. You will have to determine what's fair to charge for your shop.

If your phone call to the check bouncer doesn't produce results, you could contact the bank to see if funds are now available in the account and run the check through the banking system again. Another option when the customer ignores your phone call is to send a registered letter. The letter is written as a confirmation of the phone call and gives the check customer another 48 hours to make good on the check. If you still do not get a response a second letter is sent, by registered mail, return receipt requested explaining firmly what action the shop intends to take if reimbursement is not received.

NOTE: *Examples of return check letters are included in the Appendix A – Business Forms.*

If you do not get a response, you should file a complaint with the county district attorney office, documenting your attempts to recover the money. Call the office and ask for information, before going to the courthouse. They are usually very helpful, especially if you tell them that you represent a non-profit organization. Also the bank that you do business with can give you some pointers on dealing with returned checks. And depending upon how you view it, some shops also post the returned check offenders on their cash register reminding volunteers whom not to accept checks from, as well as alerting customers you follow up on all bounced checks.

Some shops have a "no check" policy and their sales are not affected as credit and debit cards are the preferred method of paying by most customers.

> **NOTE:** Your check cashing policy should be posted in the shop and should outline the fees you charge for all returned items.

CREDIT CARDS

In today's plastic world no matter what your volume of sales may be, you will almost have to accept credit cards for payment of purchases. If sales top $40,000 a year or more, it is really time to start accepting credit cards.

As with anything else, it is best to shop around and get recommendations since this area of finance is extremely competitive. A good place to start is the bank where you do business to see if they are affiliated with a credit card company and can offer you what is called a merchant account. Most large banks offer a small business package that includes the processing of credit card transactions, check verification, as well as the regular services for the day to day business transactions of a gift shop. Although the fees may be slightly higher than if you purchase them all ala carte, by far this is the most convenient way to go about getting the services and equipment needed to take credit cards.

But also check around with other volunteer shops in your area for information on which they use. Typically a bank will charge a setup fee, a transaction fee for each credit card transaction, as well as a percentage on each sale. Some companies even charge a monthly statement fee as well as daily reconciliation fees, so it pays to shop around or even negotiate with the prospective supplier.

You will need a separate phone line for the terminal used to verify the credit card. This too, may be an additional expense. Some companies require you buy a terminal, while others charge a monthly rental fee, while still some others may give you the use of the terminal free. Each terminal operates differently so make sure step-by-step instructions for processing credit cards in the gift shop are posted close by and also included in the manual.

The terminal doesn't always have to be a separate gadget. Rather it can be programmed into a cash register that interfaces with a modem or it can be used on a computer connected to the financial institution by way of modem or the Internet, or as most shops and restaurants use, by a separate terminal. Again there are setup fees fee for connecting the terminal, modem or POS systems, along with monthly processing fee and transaction fees. And believe me, the amounts vary widely. Any organization with a good credit history should have no problem securing a merchant account for processing credit cards.

Make sure whatever you do, when you decide to accept credit cards, realize although it's more convenient for the customer, it adds additional expense (sometimes upwards of 5% per sale). For some shops that means they raise prices slightly on those items that are typical "credit card transactions" to compensate for the expense.

LAY-A-WAYS

With credit cards being so widely used these days, lay-a-ways aren't as popular as they once were, but are still a worthwhile payment option for many customers. If you've never tried lay-a-ways, here's how they work. The customer selects merchandise to be purchased. Instead of the customer walking out the door, the merchandise is held in the gift shop's storage until the customer can pay for it in full. This ensures the customer gets what she wants, at the price she wants, but simply doesn't get it right away.

The downside to lay-a-ways is that this method of selling merchandise is time consuming for the shop attendants and bookkeepers and the shop must have adequate storage space to store the merchandise. Detailed forms for a lay-a-ways must be filled out. Transaction copies are given to the customer at the time of the initial transaction and when each lay-a-way payment is made. So, like credit cards, there is an addition hidden expense you must realize.

Typically, most shops don't accept lay-a-ways for under $25.00. And most require the down payment to be 25% of the purchase price including tax. The advantage here is that you have 25% of the money now. But the downside again is that the merchandise needs to be boxed securely and will take up space in storage. If the customer does not pay off and claim the merchandise put on lay-a-way within the date allotted, then you should attempt to contact them by phone.

If you get no response, send a certified letter explaining that the merchandise will be returned to stock on a specific date. If there is still no response within a certain period of time, you can then return the item to stock, and keep the 25%. Complete instructions for lay-a-way forms along with a blank Lay-a-way form can be found in *Appendix A - Business Forms*.

EMPLOYEE PAYROLL DEDUCTION

Another form or method of payment and an excellent way to boost your sales is employee payroll deductions. The administration of the organization and the board of directors of your volunteer organization needs to decide if they want to take on employee payroll deductions. If they do, you now have a potential customer base that is guaranteed to pay.

This is how employee payroll deductions typically work: a paid employee of the organization where you are volunteering makes a purchase in the shop. Paperwork is filled out, and is sent to the payroll department of the organization. The amount of the purchase is then deducted from the employee's paycheck. For expensive items sometimes the amount of purchase can be spread over several pay periods, and each pay period a certain amount is deducted until the purchase is paid off. Oftentimes you can set a minimum purchase amounts (typically $25) and a minimum deduction per pay period, an example being 25% of the total purchase.

Oftentimes the payroll department has guidelines for such deductions. Employees may purchase any number of items at one time to be added together for an employee payroll deduction transaction. But oftentimes, only one purchase can be made at a time, meaning each employee payroll purchase must be paid off before another can be made.

Although most plans set up payment over time, the employee payroll deduction purchase can be paid in full at any time. Keep in mind that this will be extra work for the volunteers attending the shop (and for the payroll department) and you must provide extra training to make sure everyone understands the procedure. You certainly don't want to confuse the payroll department with sloppy paperwork. Therefore, all instructions explaining the recording of the transaction and the bookkeeping should be in the shop's manual.

The shop manager and shop bookkeeper should get together with the payroll department to set up the instructions for the manual. The manual should also have instructions in the cash register operations section on how to enter the employee payroll deduction in the register. Even though this may seem like a lot of work it is popular with the employees and a great sales booster. It makes it easier for employees to buy and gives you a great way to advertise sales, if you can convince payroll to include flyers in the paycheck envelopes.

NOTE: An example of Employee Payroll Deduction instructions in Gift Shop Manual, Chapter 5 and sample contract in Appendix A - Business Forms.

Regardless of all the payment methods you offer, every gift shop should offer gift certificates for sale. But most shops fail to capitalize on such added sales options because they fail to advertise gift certificates are available. Don't loose potential sales. Post a big sign in the shop notifying customers you offer gift certificates and that they make great gifts for those hard to buy for customers.

Gift certificates make a great alternative to the customer unable to make up their mind on what to buy, and give the volunteers another method for promoting the shop. Your certificate should be attractively printed on decorated paper and come with an envelope. Such certificates can be purchased at an office supply shop or easily designed on the computer.

You should decide on the minimum amount you want to offer, such as $10. And you should keep track of the certificates through a numbered gift certificate receipt book, complete with receipt and two carbons. The information should be completely filled out, so that you can ensure no one tries to pass off bogus certificates. For example, typically one copy is given to the customer with the certificate; the second copy is used as receipt for cash register entry. The cash register section of your shop's manual should explain how to enter a certificate purchase. The printed certificate is neatly filled out, and the number from the receipt book is included. Never give a customer a blank certificate.

When redeeming a gift certificate, the customer would present the gift certificate at the time the purchase is made. The volunteer shop attendant would then match the certificate with the gift certificate receipt book. No cash or change should be given for a certificate. The cash register section of the Gift Shop manual should have instructions on how to enter the purchase paid for with a gift certificate.

IN-HOUSE CHARGES

Many small shops offer in-house charges. Although plenty of shops do fine with in-house charges, I don't advise the use of them. Why? To keep track of charges, and to send out monthly statements, means extra paperwork and unless yours is a large shop with a lot of sophisticated computer equipment and a lot of help, it's just proves to be a lot of hassle. These days people have plenty of other options to pay for their purchases.

TAX EXEMPT PURCHASES

Finally one thing to note is that from time to time you will have someone come in requesting to make a tax-exempt purchase. The person making a tax-exempt purchase <u>must</u> give the shop attendant the name and address of the tax-exempt organization or business and the tax-exempt number they are making the purchase for, at the time of purchase. The person making the purchase should present an identification card with this information, and if the purchase is for the individual who lives in a tax exempt state, they must present their state's drivers license for verification. The sale is entered into the register as tax exempt or "non tax", and the identification number should accompany the sale in a log book.

Chapter 12
Twelfth Step: Promoting the Business

To promote your gift shop you will need to communicate to the public with market communications. These communications consist of printed material, publicity, displays, paid advertising and Internet web sites. Increasing awareness with these promotional tactics will increase your traffic thereby increasing sales. Promoting your merchandise and services by forms of marketing communications not only increases sales, it is a courtesy to your customers

PRINTED MATERIALS

Printed materials include letterheads, business cards, pamphlets, brochures, fliers, table toppers, show cards and signs used in the shop. Printed material such as letterhead and business cards should have a logo or emblem, name of the volunteer organization, address, phone, fax, e-mail, web site, and the business hours.

Brochures/pamphlets printed for a gift shop should include all of the above, besides a list of merchandise and services. For example, a hospital gift shop may print a brochure to be included in the hospital information package as the patient checks in, listing convenience items available for purchase in the gift shop. The phone order instructions for room delivery should be included in the brochure. A zoo shop might print a list of all the different species of animals and related gifts that may be purchased in the shop; this would be educational as well as promoting sales. The zoo brochure could be given at the time of ticket purchase or printed on the back of the zoo's map. Museum shops could list the dates of exhibits along with suggestions for gift purchases in their shop, such as note cards with prints of old master paintings,

Flyers are usually a one-page advertisement announcing sales, new merchandise or other information pertinent to the shop. The fliers could be distributed to the different departments in the institution/facility through the in-house mail, as well as to the public as handouts or in a mailing.

Table toppers are just small signs, usually printed on cardstock. The table toppers could be put at the reception or information desk, on tables in a cafeteria, and in waiting rooms. They alert the customer with information on specific merchandise or sales and other promotions. Table toppers can be made to look professional when printed on the computer. If your computer does not take card stock, print out a master copy on regular computer paper and run the card stock through the copy machine, making your table topper.

Showcards are to give information to the customer about merchandise in the shop. It can include the price, size, styles, features and colors available. The showcard is usually used to enhance a display. More information on the use of a showcard is included in the display section of this chapter.

Signs displayed inside or outside the shop, are a necessary form of business promotion. The signs can be located just out side the shop, in the elevator cases, or in strategic locations in the building where the shop is located. Permission from the building manager is necessary. The sign should have all the pertinent information regarding the event. Signs besides being placed in-house can be put in other business in the community.

PAID ADVERTISING

What type of paid advertising is worth the money spent? The information that attracts the customer, of course. Advertising could be in your local community newspapers, travel magazines, and those magazines distributed to hotel and motels, especially if your shop is located in a museum, zoo or other tourist type attraction. In order for any of this type of advertising to be effective, it must target the customers that will frequent the shop. Here are a few examples:

- A hospital shop ad placed in a community newspaper listing gifts that could be ordered by phone and sent to a patient's room. (The shop's competitive pricing on the variety of gifts available was mentioned. The offer of free and speedy delivery, if the shop can provide this service, was included. Don't forget the direct phone number of the shop, as well as the shop's business hours.)
- A museum shop ad placed in travel magazine highlighting gifts pertaining to art collections currently on display.
- A municipal park gift shop ad placed in a travel magazine to advertise area souvenirs that could be purchased in their gift shop with the location and pertinent information about the shop.

There is a misconception among some volunteer organizations that since they represent a non-profit or charitable organization that they cannot advertise. The volunteer organization may place paid advertisements in newspapers and magazines as long as the organization you represent has given approval.

An advertisement will promote a sale or special event, build a favorable image and gain recognition for the shop. The ad should focus on the needs and desires of your targeted customer and emphasize the benefits the customer will derive from patronizing the shop. If you can save the customer time and money, say so. If you can provide an item or service not readily found at other retail shops, say so.

Even though creating effective advertising is an art that requires special writing and artistic skills, the inexperienced person with a little talent, a computer and the basic suggestions listed, can create an enticing ad that will bring customers to your shop. A photograph of the organization's building or of the gift shop mentioning items sold in the shop, the services offered, competitive prices, address, directions, phone and credit cards accepted will attract customers.

It is advisable to check with the administration of the institution/facility and the board of the volunteer organization you represent before submitting any advertisement to any media. Most community newspapers will give a volunteer (non-profit) organization a special rate.

INTERNET ADVERTISING

While not necessary for the success of a gift shop, the web site, in today's technology world, is an asset. It will not only get the name of your organization to the public, it may attract new customers and increase sales. It's the way to advertise in the 2000's. Many hospital and museum shops already have their own web sites. Your volunteer organization may already have a site and your shop could add a link to the existing site.

Do not disregard this as too costly or too technical as you will be surprised at how easy and inexpensive it is to create a web site. You will want to decide, first, what image you want to project and what you want to communicate to the viewer of the site. Do you just want to make people aware of the shop with the location, hours, etc. or do you want to show the merchandise offered for sale? Only you know what you have and what your customers clamor for.

A web site would be valuable for the hospital shop as the viewers could see the type of flower arrangements and prices and could make their purchase from home. The museum shop could display the type of artwork in the shop. A shop in a municipal park could show souvenirs exclusive to their shop.

Now for the software and tools needed in setting up the site. I am assuming that you have already purchased your computer and by now are getting proficient with the desk top publishing program. So we will start from there. If you know how to use a word processor you can create a web page.

If you intend on using photographs on the web site you will need a flat bed or digital scanner. Scanners convert regular photos into digital images. As of this writing, the cost of a scanner is nominal, less than $100. Keep in mind that a scanner could be useful in other projects that the volunteer organization may be involved in. Look for a scanner that has at least 600X1200 pixels (dots) per inch. If you don't think you can afford a scanner at this time but still want to use photos in your web page, have the film of regular photos you have taken with a regular camera put on a computer disk. The images of the photos on this disk can be downloaded to your web site. The cost of having your film processed on the disk is around $6.

If your shop intends to create a catalog of the shop's merchandise on the web site you may think about investing in a digital camera.

The organization's logo, slogan or emblem should be included in the web site. You may want to show pictures of the shop. Include all information that you would include in a printed brochure about the shop. Be sure to include the detailed instructions for making a phone order, etc. Try to keep it simple, as it is really a turn off (computer turn off) when you have to go through a lot of steps and wait for the screen to slowly change, when you are visiting a web site. Remember your objective is to let your customer know what you have for sale.

Note: For more information on how to set up a simple web site or for a qualified certified web site developer, go to www.frustrateduser.com.

PUBLICITY

Publicity the best form of advertising, is free and requires little effort on your part, just some media 'inside information' to attract an editors attention. Publicity for your shop could be tied in with the election of new officers or board members, awards to volunteers, remodeling, expansion, relocation, special events, fund raisers, raffles, contest, volunteer recruitment, public service information or unique merchandise in the shop. It could be a feature story about the philanthropic works the organization made possible by the sales in the gift shop.

Sometimes a local newspaper will approach a volunteer organization for newsworthy items, but if you feel you have an event that would make a good news story, this is how to initiate this publicity. You will have to attract the attention of the media in the form of a press release. The way you introduce yourself to the newspaper depends on the size of the newspaper. If it is a large metropolitan newspaper, you should write a letter of introduction; if the newspaper is a small community paper you could phone the editor or introduce yourself in person. You could also post free press releases on such web sites as PRweb.com.

Either way you will want to convey to the editor that from time to time you will be submitting press releases from your organization and gift shop and you would like to know the procedures that would help conform to the editor's requirements. Ask about deadlines. Make sure that the release is sent to the proper address. Your best chance of getting your press release printed is to address it to the appropriate editor.

To write a press release that will attract attention you will need to follow some of the rules in the newspaper business. It should be printed on a standard 8 1/2" X11" paper. Use the organization's stationary with letterhead if available, with margins of 3/4" to 1". Keep the release to one page. The words "NEWS" and "FOR IMMEDIATE RELEASE" (or release date) should appear near the top of the page. It should be dated. The headlines should be in all capital letters.

The body of the release should be double-spaced. A contact name, phone and email address should be included. At the end of the release, type the word "end" or the number signs "###". This is the trades' way of indicating the end of the release. If you just have to have more than one page type "more" at the end of the first page and continue to the second page. Keep all sentences and paragraphs short. Make the headline catchy but to the point. The first paragraph should be an attention grabber.

Do not offer opinions but do include quotes from those people in your organization or customers who have something to say. The release should be written in a journalistic style, with the most important information at the beginning. Information for release should answer the questions who, what, where, when, why and how. Keep in mind that the news release is to attract the attention of the editor. If you send a photo, it should be either 5"X7" or 8"X10" black and white glossy. Captions attached to the photo should be readable from the front of the photo. Because your release may be printed verbatim in a newspaper spend ample time to include only the important information in a clever and concise story. Have someone proof read the release before sending and check to see that names are spelled correctly. A sample news release is then mailed to the local paper (An example is in *Appendix A - Business Forms*.)

After an appropriate length of time, make a follow up phone call to the editor to make sure they received your release, asking if you can provide any additional information.

Do not be pushy and do not call to complain if they do not run the release. Just wait a month and try another release, maybe with a different angle.

The more releases you send, the more likely one of them will eventually be printed. Don't get discouraged. Just keep trying. With persistence and patience, a newsworthy community oriented story will get printed.
In some cases your news release may be just the enticement for a feature story on the shop. Then the editor will send out a reporter to write up a story. You must make sure that you give the reporter information to make the story appealing, something to entice the public into the shop, to bring in the curious shopper that probably had no intention of making a visit to shop's organization. It would be a good idea to have two or three other volunteers on hand besides the manager, when the newspaper conducts the interview. What one person doesn't think of the other one will! Remember nothing is really said "off the record". Be completely accurate, do not exaggerate, exacerbate or aggravate. It is astounding what a little free publicity will do to increase the volume of traffic in the shop.

After your news release or feature article is printed, send thank-you notes to the editor and reporter. Besides showing your appreciation for the publicity, this will make your shop memorable for the next news release. Suggested reading on the subject of publicity "The New Publicity Kit" by Jeanette Smith. This is an excellent book for nonprofit organization that covers it all.

SALES PROMOTIONS
Sales promotions are ways to get more traffic in your shop. Having reduction or close out sales are forms of promoting sales. You can also promote sales with free samples, offers, coupons, contest, drawings, introductory offers, free refreshments, free gifts, and logo souvenirs.

Sales or reductions of merchandise should be only on rare occasions. The volunteer operated shop should have only one or two sales a year to get rid of damaged, dated and dud merchandise. While a sale is the standard way the retail shop attracts customers, is not a good promotion for the volunteer shop. Merchandise is usually customized to these types of shops, the needs and desires of the particular customers that patronize these types of shops are identified and merchandise is purchased accordingly, so there should be few duds.

The shop is not working if there is a need for a lot of reduction sales as a business promotion to lure customers.

Here are some ideas and examples of promotions that have worked in a variety of gift shops. Consider trying some or all of these if your sales are slumping:

- Samples for the customer such as potpourri, fragrances, soaps, candy or cookies that are sold in the shop
- Offers could be merchandise not readily found in the area, rare merchandise or lower price offer on a particular item
- Coupons for a percentage off or a free item with a minimum purchase.
- Contest relating to the organization's function
- Drawings for a limited edition or unusual item
- Introductory offer of a new item on the market, preferably a collectable item or jewelry items that need added accessories will insure more sales
- Free refreshment, free gift, logo imprinted souvenirs and other give-a-ways are other ways to get a potential customer in the shop and present an obligation to make a purchase

DISPLAYS

Displaying merchandise is a form of merchandising that is often overlooked in the volunteer shop. Usually the merchandise items are just lined up on selves and no thought is given to arrangement or displaying.

Display is visual selling and in the volunteer shop, it accounts for approximately 1 in 5 sales. The average shopper's eyes spend 10 seconds viewing a display for the first time. The average shopper makes a decision on what and how much to buy based on the merchandise itself, where it is positioned within the store and on the shelf, and how effectively it is displayed. So it is imperative that your displays attract attention. You will want to create exciting store environments and display merchandise so that more customers stop, look, touch, and buy.

I will include in this chapter ways to create dynamic, attention-grabbing displays on a limited budget.

The first step is to fine tune the shop's layout to improve traffic flow. This will maximize merchandise exposure. Then plan your displays using signs, props, and effective lighting to make displays come alive and attract customer attention.

Think about the purpose of the display. Is it to feature a new item or maybe highlight a slow moving item?

A good display publicizes merchandise and tells the customer what is available for sale.

In a well designed display the merchandise is the main focus.

The elements of display are:

- The area (windows, shelves, etc.)
- The merchandise selection
- Props
- Sign & showcards
- Lighting

Your displays will consist of window displays, shelf and counter displays, floor and wall displays. Every square inch of the shop is on display.

The window display attracts and draws in the customer. The window display should have a theme, motif or impart a message. Interior displays should sell the merchandise.

After you have decided on a window or shelf location for a display, the merchandise and props are selected. In the volunteer shop, space is crucial and does not allow for large props. You want to devote what space you have for salable merchandise, what you have plenty of, in stock.

Remember when using props that they should not dominate but compliment or enhance the merchandise. Clearly mark on the bottom of the prop that it is "not for sale". Never put a prop in a display that you cannot part with. Invariably someone will request to purchase it and may offer a price you cannot refuse. When it comes to props...keep it simple. You do not want to detract from the merchandise for sale. You want to attract attention to the merchandise you are trying to sell. You do not want the merchandise to be cluttered with props. This just confuses the customer and can kill a sale.

Suggested props include a crate, wagon, cart, cradle, antiques, easel, screen, bricks, logs, baker's rack, basket, book, ladder, artificial plant.

When placing the merchandise, you may want to include only like items in your display or the items of the same color. Your display may consist of only holiday merchandise or merchandise with a certain theme.

To insure addition sales, arrange the shop to maximize impulse sales. For example, put gift bags and enclosure cards near the cash register. Position the candy and gum displays at the check-out counter.

Now for the mechanics that go into making a display pleasing to the eye…remember the sizes of the items in the display should be consistent and in proportion to one another. In other words you should try to avoid placing items that are of normal size with items that are in miniature. Larger items are generally placed in the back of the display, graduating down with smaller items, allowing for the one item of merchandise to dominate. Your display should be harmonious in line, shape, size and texture.

Think of the area designated, as space to be divided into arrangements used in the display. Space divisions that will be helpful in arranging are pyramid, step, zigzag and repetition, progression of sizes and radiation. On the following page, are examples of this space division in graphic form.

Display Examples:

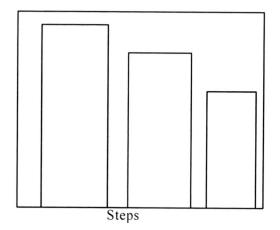
Steps

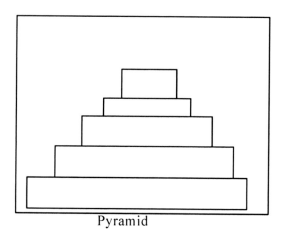
Pyramid

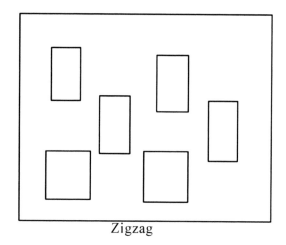
Zigzag

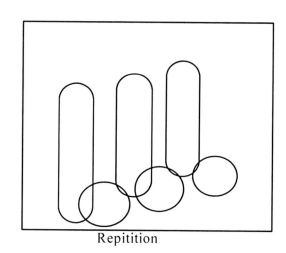
Repitition

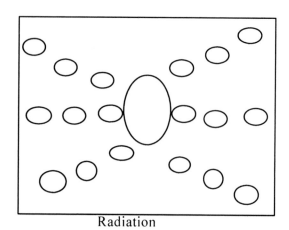
Radiation

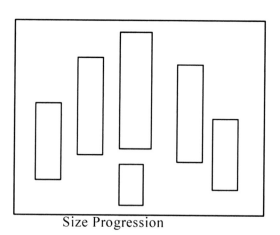
Size Progression

Placement should take into consideration that the customer will be handling the merchandise, so stacked items where one could fall and break is not a good idea. Make it safe, comfortable and convenient for the customer to handle the merchandise.

It's a good idea to place the gift box accompanying the item under the item or behind the item in the display. Most merchandise will be sold off the display, anyway. An attractive gift box appropriately placed will not detract from your displays and in some cases will add to the arrangement. It also provides needed product information. You will be surprised at how much smoother the shop will run if this one suggestion is taken. True you may not be able to get as many items on the shelves but by eliminating the frustration caused by trying to find a suitable gift box, will be worth it. Remember that most of the purchases will be gifts. It is almost impossible to come up with a system for categorizing and storing gift boxes or for using the item on the shelf as just the display and retrieving a like item from a storage room.

When arranging merchandise on the shelves, place like items together. Many of your customers have a limited amount of time to make a purchase and do not want to spend time on a scavenger hunt. So if you put all the baby items, or all the frames, or all the souvenirs, all the stuffed animals, etc. together, your customer will appreciate it.

Showcards are necessary for displays in a non-profit shop but remember:

- ✓ While visible information about a product helps sell, you don't want to clutter the shelves with printed information,
- ✓ That showcards speak for the display and act as a silent salesperson, answering the customers questions.
- ✓ That showcards are a very important selling tool in the volunteer shop.
- ✓ Showcards are a necessary part of any display.
- ✓ That the showcards can relate the mission of the host institution.

Showcards are just another addition to your visual selling. Attractive and professional showcards can be made on the computer, using card stock.

Lighting in the display is also important. Here's a list of things to ensure:

- ✓ Make sure that the jewelry case is lighted.
- ✓ Remember that glassware looks best when the light is at the back of the display.
- ✓ Use spotlights just on selected merchandise and don't overdo spots.
- ✓ Make sure that a display light does not shine directly into the customer's eyes or create a glare.

Color

Color plays an important part in your display, too. Color has an effect on the emotions of your customer. Color can convey a holiday, seasonal and merchandise theme. Here are some ideas when and how to use colors.

Color	Emotional Effect	Theme
White	pure, celestial	Winter, snow, angels Mother's Day, Christmas
Yellow	cheerful, inspiring	Summer, Easter
Orange	energy, warmth	Fall, Halloween, Thanksgiving
Red	exciting, passionate	Christmas, Valentines 4th of July, patriotic
Pink	lively, youthful	Mother's Day, baby display
Purple	mystery, dignified, rich royal, jewelry display	Easter,
Blue	calming, cool	Patriotic, water display baby display
Green	relaxing, refreshing	St. Patrick's Day money, nature display
Black	emptiness, mourning	Halloween, accents, frightening
Brown	earthy	Fall, nature display

Using a variety of color will draw attention to the shop. Color will help convey a theme or mood. It will draw the customer into the shop. As you select merchandise to sell in the shop in various colors to appeal to different customer taste, you will want to select colors of merchandise to display to appeal to those varieties of taste. Remember that a good display will help sell the merchandise. Anyone can learn how to make an attractive display with these few basic guidelines.

Keep the displays dusted, clean and organized!

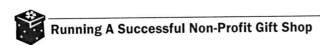

CHAPTER 13
Thirteenth Step: Measuring Your Success

The shop has been in operation for 6 months, the merchandise has been selling and money is coming in. Things seem to be operating smoothly. But how are you really doing? Measuring your success is not something you should do, but something you have to do! But how do you go about it? There are many methods used in business to determine the successes and failures of a business. These methods are in the form of statements, formulas and ratios. There are statements required to report the net worth of the shop and to report the profits or losses. There are formulas to determine cost of merchandise. There are ratios to calculate ultimate space usage and ratios that tell you the percentage of profit you earn on sales. In this chapter I will show you ways to use the methods for measuring that are applicable to this type of gift shop.

TAKING AN INVENTORY

When you first opened the shop merchandise was purchased to sell. This was your beginning inventory. In order to find out how the shop has done over the past year or accounting period, take an inventory of the merchandise that is remaining in the shop... the merchandise still left in the shop, to be sold. This cost of the merchandise left at the end of the accounting period is then subtracted from the cost of the merchandise that you started out with. This will give you the cost of the merchandise that has been sold. With this cost of the merchandise sold (Cost of Goods Sold – COGS) you will create the financial statements and use it in the formulas and ratios to determine how the shop is doing.

This physical inventory should be taken at least once a year. A count is taken of each item in stock, and I do mean each and every item! The physical inventory also tells if you have shortages due to theft, shoplifting, poor record keeping or shortages in shipments. The physical inventory is necessary for financial reporting and can also reveal important information about mistakes in purchasing.

*NOTE: All inventories are valued at **cost**.*

It is a good idea to prepare ahead of time for the inventory. A month, before, you should:

- Straighten and organize the storeroom
- Let the stock on low profit items dwindle
  (This includes things like greeting cards, candy and gum and sundry items.)
- Hold a pre-inventory sale of all the shopworn and slow moving merchandise
- Delay the delivery of any new purchases until after inventory
  You may have old stock in the storeroom. Don't hold on to these items that are not selling. Put them on sale! Slow moving merchandise can be written down if it has been on the inventory for a year and in some cases 6 months.

Inform your staff of the date you plan to do the inventory and ask for volunteers. About a week before you start your count, go through the shop and start breaking up displays to put like items together. This will make counting go faster. Post the inventory dates a week prior to remind the volunteers and offer an incentive such as a free lunch for those who participate. If it is not possible to take the inventory after shop hours, I'd recommend closing the shop on the day or days of inventory. You should give everyone counting the inventory an inventory form.

This form lists the quantity, description of item, selling price and cost. (You will find an inventory form in *Appendix A - Business Forms*- In Closing & Forms.) Make enough copies of the inventory form for each department in the shop. Make sure you have enough sharpened pencils, clipboards, calculators and refreshments. (These instructions are for taking an inventory manually. If you have a POS system your inventory will be taken by scanning the barcodes on each item in the shop. You will have to secure the scanners and instructions from the company that provided your system for the persons taking the inventory.)

Tips for taking inventory:

1. At the top of page designate type of inventory (Example "Greeting Cards")
2. Under description describe the type (birthday, etc.). Make your description brief.
3. Include the name of the manufacturer or company if possible.
4. Include the retail price and the number of items in stock.
5. Cost and extension should be calculated later. During inventory all you want to do is get a description/with item # and a count of all the items in the shop.

An example of an inventory form showing you how to use the form:

Type of Inventory ___Jewelry_____ *Page* _1___ *of* _1___

Item #	Description	Retail Price	Quantity	Cost	Extension
10056	Angel Earring pierced	$8.99	3	4.00	12.00
10136	Heart Earring Pierced	$10.00	5	5.00	25.00
10299	Angel Earring Clip	$8.99	4	4.00	16.00

*Page Total*_____

*Previous Page Total*_____

*TOTAL*_____

Methods of Measuring

There's no doubt, comparing your gift shop with average standards will inspire you to set your goals high and to strive to achieve them. Businesses use ratios and formulas to find out how they are doing, what they have done, and where they are going. These ratios are also used to make comparisons.

The formula used in business to determine cost of sales and profit on sales is called the "Cost of Goods Sold" **COGS.** This cost is imperative in generating the financial statements and is necessary for calculating the methods of measuring. An inventory count is used in determining the cost of goods sold.

The beginning inventory, the merchandise that you started out the year or accounting period with, is added to the cost of all the merchandise purchases made during the year. The ending inventory is subtracted from this amount giving you the COGS (total cost of goods sold). Now the COGS is subtracted from the total gross sales for the year, resulting in the gross profit for the year. Here is that formula outlined in detail below:

Beginning Inventory

+Purchases

-Ending Inventory

=COGS

Gross Sales

-COGS

=Gross Profit

(All the information gathered to find the COGS will be part of your income statement. A sample Income Statement along with a Balance Sheet are in *Appendix A - Business Forms*. These 2 financial statements should be generated at the end of each accounting period. They should be made available to all the volunteers and the facility/institution where the shop is operated. You will need these financial statements when filing the federal return.)

Now that an inventory has been taken and you have arrived at a Cost of Goods Sold. with the COGS formula, you have the information necessary for making other measurements....the ratio. Ratio analysis is an excellent method for calculating the overall financial condition of your gift shop. It puts the information from a financial statement into perspective.

Sales per Square Foot of Selling Space

For example, to determine how you are doing in sales for the size of your particular shop, use this simple ratio - divide the total square feet of your shop into the gross annual retail sales. This result of this ratio will equal the average sales per square foot in dollars. It's this average that will gauge how well you're doing compared to nationwide averages.

Sales/Shop Square Footage = Sales per Square Foot

For instance, say your total sales at retail for the past 6 months have been $100,000 and the square footage of your shop is 425. Assuming your sales for the next 6 months will be another $100,000, divide 425 into $200,000. The result tells you that for every square foot of space in the shop you're generating sales of $470 per year. This figure not only tells you what to expect for future sales, but is also a good indicator to determine if you are using the space in the shop effectively.

The average shop utilizing space effectively and managing efficiently will be somewhere between $400 and $500. If your results fall within those figures, consider yourself a success. If not, and yours are lower, that just means you have something to strive for. Find ways to use your floor space more effectively.

Merchandise Turnover

A ratio used in measuring success is the Inventory Turnover Ratio. How fast is the turnover of the merchandise in the gift shop? How many times a year do you have to reorder new merchandise? The way to determine how fast your merchandise sells and needs to be replaced is with the inventory turnover ratio. It is really a measure of how hard your inventory *dollars* are working for you, by how often each inventory dollar is used per year to buy merchandise.

When we think about inventory turn over it is easier to visualize how many times we have reordered certain merchandise than it is to visualize dollars being reused to buy that merchandise.

The measurement of inventory turn over is an important calculation but like so many calculations, if the data is inaccurate, or the calculation is wrong or applied inconsistently, the result is useless. This measurement is one of the hardest business formulas to understand. In the next section, I'll explain it step-by-step and show you how the calculation works

.

There are variations as to how turnover should be calculated, but the one formula I've used for the vast majority of applications is this:

COGS/Average Inventory at Cost +Inventory Turnover

How do you get the formula to work? First, gather the information you need to make the calculation. Here's how you'd find out each piece:

Annual Cost of Goods Sold $ _____

The Annual Cost of Goods Sold is the total cost of goods purchased over a twelve-month period.

Average Inventory at Cost $ _____

Considering the seasonality of many stores, and that inventory is generally taken infrequently, the calculation of an average inventory can be difficult.

- If you take an inventory at high season and another at low season, average the two.
- If you take two inventories a year you can actually use three inventories (1. Last year's final inventory; 2. The current year's mid-year inventory; 3. The final inventory from this year) and divide by three.
- If you take only one inventory don't use an inventory taken when the stock on hand is extremely low, which will result in an inaccurate, high number of turns, and don't discount your performance by using a large inventory number resulting in a low number of turns. If you are like most stores and take only one inventory a year, adjust that inventory number to reflect your best estimate of your average inventory.
- If you take only one inventory a year you can also take the ending inventory from the previous year and the most recent inventory and divide by two.
- If you are busy only seven months (and very, very slow for the remaining five months) then your average inventory should primarily reflect your average inventory levels during the busy season.

Now, do the calculation.

If you have gathered the information carefully, the easy calculation results in an accurate and useful number. For example if your annual COGS was $150,000 your average inventory during the year was $45,000, simply divide the Annual Cost of Goods Sold ($150,000) by the Average Inventory at Cost ($45,000).

150,000/45,000=3.33

The answer, 3.33 inventory turns, indicates that you used your inventory dollars 3.33 times during the twelve months being measured and the inventory turned over 3.33 times.

Please note two things. First, both numbers used for the calculation are at *cost*. While it is typical to use cost numbers you can use retail numbers. The important point is that the numbers must have the same base — cost or retail. Second, it is typical to base this calculation on annual numbers.

Square footage is also a factor affecting turns. A shop that is too big may have slower turns because it requires too much inventory to keep the shop looking full and inviting. A shop that is too small my have elevated turns because it needs to be re-stocked more frequently.

In general, the higher the turns the better. High turns mean you are using your inventory dollars efficiently, your stock looks fresher, and you probably need less storage space. If the turns are too low however, too much capital is being tied up in inventory and the store may be short of cash that can be used to buy newer merchandise.

> *Note*: Generally, a high inventory turnover is an indicator of good inventory management. But a high ratio can also mean there is a shortage of inventory.

A low turnover may indicate overstocking, or obsolete inventory.

COGS %

And another percentage evaluation/ratio is the cost of goods sold ratio. This percent is the cost of merchandise purchased that has been sold. To find this percentage simply divide the cost of goods sold by gross sales.

COGS/Gross Sales = COGS %

Try to keep the cost of your good sold in the shop as low as possible. Consider putting to use the buying tips I've outlined in Chapter 9. The COGS percentage should stay below 55% if everything is run right!

Determining the Bottom Line! (Ratio)

But remember that sales and how fast the inventory is sold are not the most important concerns in a business. In this day and age, outward appearances aren't everything. A shop can have fabulously high sales but have a low net profit. Sales, in this case, do not mean a thing. A shop can have a high rate of merchandise turn over, but still not make profit. Actually the most important thing is **profit on sales**.
Profit is the bottom-line!

Gross Profit/Gross Sales = Gross Profit %

If the shop is run entirely by volunteers and most of your expenses are paid for by the organization, then your net profit percentage or margin should be at least 40%. There are a number of factors that should be considered when arriving at these percentages. For example, does the shop pay rent? Do you have any paid employees? Do you pay for operating expenses such as postage, telephone, supplies, printing/copying, maintenance, bank and credit card fees? Does the shop pay the sales tax? Does the organization that you volunteer for pay for or provide most of the cost of operations that just listed? Get the idea?

If the shop pays rent on occupied space then the profit margin ideally should be between 35% and 40%. Shops with paid managers should have at least a 40% profit margin. A good paid manager should be able to increase sale enough to maintain this profit margin and in essence pay for themselves. Any volunteer managed shop paying most of the operating expenses should have a 40% profit margin or higher. Most all volunteer operated shops I've worked with, without many expenses, typically maintain between a 45% to 55% profit margin. Again, these are conservative figures for profit in this type of situation. If your shop is not near these percentages, you should look at your shop in more detail to find the cause. Of course if you're in a very competitive market, with a less-focused hook, then your margin will be lower. But if you are the only gift shop, in a one-of-a-kind museum, then your profit margin should be up in the 40% or more range.

FIANCIAL REPORTING

Now you have gathered all this information, you have counted, calculated and evaluated. You know how you are doing. Now it is time to report your findings. The reports are statements of your financial conditions - the balance sheet and the income statement.

The balance sheet lists the shops assets, liabilities and net worth. If you are just starting out and opening a new shop, you should prepare an "Start-up Balance Sheet" listing the cost of equipment or any construction cost your volunteer organization has incurred. You will use this as a worksheet to gather information to prepare your initial balance sheet.

The income statement, also referred to as a profit and loss statement, shows all the income and expenses during a certain period. The expenses are subtracted from income to arrive at a profit or loss for that period.

These statements will show just how you are doing. You can now see how keeping track of sales, taking an inventory, finding your cost of goods sold fits in to arriving at a profit.

The volunteer organization and the host organization will require these statements at least once during an accounting period (fiscal or calendar year). You will need these statements when filing tax returns.

You will find an example of a balance sheet and an income statement in Appendix A – Business Forms. These statements were prepared just for the gift shop in a non-profit setting.

MORE IDEAS FOR ADDED PROFIT

So you've priced the items right, you've checked your costs of goods sold, you have tried standard methods for promoting sales, but what else can you do to increase profits? Since you're volunteering your time anyway, you might as well go that extra mile to increase your profits for your charitable cause. Isn't that what it's all about? Here are my list of ideas I've used for purchasing merchandise, and soliciting donations that will add to your bottom line. I have included fund-raising ideas the shop could sponsor. Here are some suggestions:

1. Implementing the various marketing ideas found in Chapter 12 to get the customers in the shop.

2. Offering employee payroll deduction purchases. Offering more purchase options can increase sales by as much as 15%

3. Offer a discount to each employee on their birthday. Cards could be sent out wishing them "Happy Birthday" with the amount of the discount in the shop.

4. Reevaluate your pricing. Sometimes bringing up prices actually bring up sales, and also increase profit margins. You may need to adjust the mark-ups on various items. That's where watching sales closely will help you determine the right pricing structure.

5. Buy more for less. Try to find desirable merchandise at closeout prices below cost then charge the regular retail price in the shop. Buying at 'close-out' or 'going out of business' sales require time and the experience of a savvy shopper familiar with the wholesale cost of the merchandise.

6. Buy out of season merchandise at 66% to 90% at retail shops. This percentage mark-down is below wholesale cost.
(I know a hospital gift shop buyer that scouts the sale racks in infant departments of large department stores for out of season outfits for newborns. When she considers that there is no shipping cost and that this type of merchandise does not take up a lot of storage space and the fact that she will purchase the items below cost, she knows that this is a good buy and will help increase profits.) When purchasing from a retailer for resale, purchase items that have a deep mark down and will not take up a lot of storage space. And this goes without saying, only purchase merchandise that is presentable for resale, Items that are not shopworn or dated. Remember that you are buying for a non-profit, so if your state has a sales tax, take your tax ID number so you will not be charged the tax.)

7. Purchase from wholesale clubs, discount or dollar stores. It is a good idea to purchase a membership in your local wholesale club. You are able to purchase candy and drug and sundry items at a discount, have a wide variety of choices and are able to make a profit on the mark-up. You will be able to select perishable and dated items that are fresh. Other items I would suggest are books. You can just buy one of any title to test out your market. Fresh flowers and plants can be purchased at a discount and if you happen to have a talented flower arranger in your group even better. You can make big money by making your own flower arrangements to sell in the shop. (Ask your fellow volunteers for donations of vases. Everyone has florist vase taking up space in

their cabinets. With very little talent you can take a few long stem roses combined with fern, add a single tied bow and put into a donated bud vase. You will have about $4 dollars in an item you can resell for $10 or $12. You will be able to provide your customer with a product much less than they can purchase through a florist and have fun doing it.)

8. Shop discount or dollar store to purchase greeting cards suitable for your gift shop. You do not have to buy in volume and can select cards that will appeal to your type of customer. These cards are usually priced below wholesale cost and they are printed with the manufacturer retail cost, which will be your retail cost. Look for other souvenir type items at these shops.

9. Make 100% profit on donated items such as jewelry and books. Ask the volunteers to go through their jewelry boxes and donate jewelry they no longer want. Clean with jewelry cleaner, sterilize the earring, put on jewelry cards and have a gigantic jewelry sale in the gift shop. Add to the sale the jewelry inventory items in the shop that are not selling. Ask the volunteers for donations of paper or hard back books. Clear off a shelf in the back of the shop or put the used books on a cart just outside the entrance to the shop. This is especially profitable in a hospital setting. You could almost consider this a service to the visitor or patient by having reading materials at 'give-a-way' prices. This idea proved to be a success in a municipal garden gift shop. The members of the garden center associated with the municipal garden donated books on horticulture, gardening, landscaping, flower arranging, etc. to resell in the shop.

10. Ask the retail gift shops in your community for donations of items they cannot sell. During the time you were setting up the shop, you should have been in contact with the owner or manager of a "for profit" gift shop in your community asking for advice and information. (A hospital shop manger received donations from a

greeting card store manager on a regular basis. Sometimes the merchandise was seasonal, but finding storage was not a problem when it brought in 100% profit.)

11. Sell souvenir or items unique to your area in the shop. Remember the story of how a shop manager of a municipal shop, in a garden center, made money on a porcelain swan designed for the nearby Swan Lake? Well, another manager of gift shop in a hospital located in a wooded area called Woodlands Estates ran across a ceramic angel advertised in a catalog that was titled 'Woodlands Angel'. Just before Christmas, she placed an order for a dozen and ran an ad in the local newspaper advertising the angel as the 'Woodlands Estates Angel'. She ended up reordering seven times before Christmas Eve. Look for items that are unique to the area where you live. Usually you can increase the mark-up on these items.

12. Form a group composed of managers of volunteer operated or volunteer manned shops in your area within a 50 to 100 mile radius. Meet once or twice a year to exchange ideas. You can gain wealth of information and at the same time share your successes. Each meeting could be at a different shop location. This was successful in the Houston, Texas area.

13. At each major market there are usually seminars geared to volunteer operated shops that include suggestions on increasing profits. Take advantage of these. Before registering get an agenda of the topics to be presented and the qualifications of the presenter to determine if the seminar would be beneficial to take that valuable time to attend.

14. Send out Holiday mailings listing the unique gift items in the shop.

15. Plan events for members of the community. Suggestion: A Sunday afternoon tea for area business women introducing a line of bath items for sale in the shop.

The manufacturer of the products may help defray cost of the event or send a representative to demonstrate their product. Events such as this will broaden your customer base.

FUNDRAISING RAFFLE IDEAS

While most volunteer organizations have had a book or jewelry sale put on by promoter and made money for their organization, I will share other fund raising ideas that require little or no up front investment and require minimal effort in the set-up.

1. **Holiday Wreath Raffle:**

   Contact six or so florists, decorating or craft shops in your area and ask for a donation of a decorated holiday wreath. Make the initial contact by letter explaining a little bit about your organization and that you will be soliciting wreaths from a number of businesses to hold a 'holiday wreath raffle' in the lobby of your organization. Their wreath will be displayed along with the name of their business. Explain that the proceeds from the raffle will benefit a worthy cause funded by your non-profit organization. Add that the event will be publicized with a list of donors. You have nothing invested, only the hooks to hang the wreaths and a roll of raffle tickets. You also have beautiful holiday decorations for the lobby at no cost! Of course, you will have to have the approval of the administration of the institution/facility/municipality, the building superintendent and the volunteer organization.

2. Holiday Drawings:

Almost every community has a traditional scheduled holiday event. You could hold a drawing for tickets to this event. For example, if the production of "The Nutcracker" ballet is playing in your area. You could sell chances for four tickets that were donated by the promoter of the event. In the gift shop you could sell nutcrackers and maybe give a chance for the tickets with each nutcracker sold. Explain when asking the promoter for the donation of the tickets that this will be added publicity for the event.

3. Purchase souvenir type merchandise:

You can use such merchandise to sell specifically for that event or suggest that the talented volunteer in your organization design and hand craft items for such an occasion. In one community there is a Holiday event just after Thanksgiving announcing the Christmas season called the "Lighting of the Doves". The city had a ceremony to light a Christmas display in the city park The local hospital gift shop capitalized on this by enlisting all their talented volunteers to make artificial flower arrangements including candles and feather doves. They placed an ad in a local paper, called the arrangements the "Lighting of the Doves". and took orders before the event. (Many of the people in the community had parties on the night of the lighting ceremony and needed centerpieces.) The proceeds went towards the purchase of Teddy Bears to give children who were admitted to the emergency room. These holiday suggestions could be applied to other popular events through out the year in your community.

4. *High Demand Item Raffle:*

We all know that when we have a rare or 'high demands' item that a drawing is a good way to raise funds without a lot of effort. Remember those Beanie Babies? I am sure that you probably entered in a raffle or took chances on the "Princess Di" Beanie Baby Bear for your daughter or granddaughter.

CHAPTER 14
In Closing – Things to Remember

The information found in this book comes from years of my own time and effort volunteering for a variety of non-profit gift shops in both Texas and Oklahoma. My hope is that you've picked up valuable information that will help you maximize profits in your non-profit gift shop.

I'm happy to share my experiences with you. If you have any questions, please do not hesitate to contact me at any of the following options:

Email: nancykirk@houston.rr.com

WebSite: www.giftshopguide.com.

I'm here to answer any questions you have, Monday thru Friday from 9a.m to 6pm. CST.

Thanks for reading and more importantly, thanks for volunteering and in turn making this a better world! Best of luck in your endeavor!

–Nancy

Appendix A:

Business Forms

Even a small volunteer operated shop will encounter a number of occasions where a contract is needed. The small gift shop will need to carry on business correspondence just like the large retail shop in the mall. You will be receiving merchandise from vendors and suppliers. You may handle merchandise in the shop made by individuals. You will be dealing with different customer situations. You will be keeping financial records. So you will need business contracts, forms and letters.

At your local office supply store you can purchase all types of business contracts and forms, but most of these pre-printed forms are not applicable to the volunteer operated shop. During the years, I have customized contract, forms, letters and financial documents to use in the daily operations for this type of shop.

To make your life a little easier, I've included these contracts and forms for you right here in this chapter. I have also included suggestions for business correspondence that may also be helpful.

Copy the forms, spread sheets and financial statements. Fill in the blanks for use in your shop.

The contracts or letters may be edited and customized for your shop.

If you do not find what you need here, search the small business sites on line. Many contain templates for contracts and business forms.

Budget

	JAN	FEB	MAR	APR	MAY	JUN	JUL	AUG	SEP	OCT	NOV	DEC	TOTAL
Sales													
Sales tax													
Purchases													
Cards													
Gifts													
Plush													
Toys													
Jewelry													
Flowers													
Drugs/ Sundry													
Candy													
Total Purchases													
Expenses:													
Postage													
Phone													
Supplies													
Equipment													
Other													

Notes:

STATEMENT

Statement

Date: _____ *, 200__*

Customer: _____
Address: _____

_____

Date	Invoice #	Description	Amount Due

TOTAL

Thank you for shopping our Gift Shop!

All proceeds benefit _____

DAILY REPORT

#sold	Description	Price	%off Sale	Tax	Total	Total
					TOTAL	

DAILY RECONCILIATION FORM

NET SALES   _____

TAX   _____

TOTAL   _____

CREDIT CARD
SALES   _____

CHECKS   _____

CASH   _____
(LINE 3 MINUS LINES 4 AND 5)

TOTAL   _____
(SHOULD BE THE SAME AS LINE 3)

COMMENTS:

_____

MONTHLY REPORT

GIFT SHOP ACCOUNT
Date:_____through_____200__

Gift Shop Sales Deposits $ _____
Date: _____
Date: _____
Date: _____
Date: _____
Date: _____
Date: _____
Date: _____
Date: _____

Charge Card Sales for month $ _____

Total $_____

Less State Tax Due $_____

TOTAL $_____

Expenses:
List of Purchases

                                                    _____
                                                    _____
                                                    _____
                                                    _____
Phone   _____
Bank Fees   _____
Credit Card Charges   _____

Total Expenses $_____

TOTAL NET INCOME $_____

PRESS RELEASE

EDITOR
LOCAL NEWSPAPER
BOX 0000
HOMETOWN, USA 00000

For further information Contact:

_____

Phone:_____

E-mail: _____

_____

FOR IMMEDIATE RELEASE

UNIQUE GIFT SHOP

Tucked away in a small corner in the lobby of _____, is a unique gift shop. The shop is manned entirely by volunteers, with all profits going for patient care and community services.

What's unique about the _____ Gift Shop is that it offers more than just the standard aspirin, toothpaste and toiletries. The Gift Shop buyers scour all the major gift and novelty and jewelry markets bringing back some of the most unusual gift items.

Besides having a wide selection of gift ideas, the Shop is competitive not only with department shop prices but with most discount shops, dispelling the common misconception that hospital gift shops are always overpriced. Currently the shop has the lowest prices in the _____ area on the popular _____.

The Gift Shop caters to newborns with everything you could imagine for that special new family member including baby announcement, teddy bears, yard signs, and where else can you find bubble gum and chocolate cigars for that proud father. The Shop also has gift ideas for grandparents, including fresh flowers, baby frames, T-shirts, infant outfits and attractive gift baskets full of useful baby items. All at unbeatable prices!

Custom gift baskets and door decorations are available.

The shop is open week days from _____a.m. to _____p.m. and Saturday and Sunday from ___ _____ a.m. to _____p.m.
Visit the _____ web site at:
http://www_____

Purchase Order

PURCHASE ORDER

PURCHASE ORDER #

DATE

Company Name_____

Address   _____

Phone   _____
Fax   _____
Email   _____

ITEM #	DESCRIPTION	QTY	COST	EXTENSION	RETAIL

TOTAL_____

VENDOR CONTRACT:

This contract or written agreement can be done in letter form or formal contract form. You must include all expectations and obligations of both parties.

Shop Name: _____

Address: _____

_____

Phone: _____

Date: _____

Supplier: _____

Address: _____

_____

Phone: _____

Contract for _____

Supplier, _____ agrees to supply _____ _____ with _____
under the following conditions:

The merchandise will be competitively priced.
The stock will be replenished weekly___ monthly___.
The Supplier will pick up merchandise not sold after a period of ___ months.
The shop will assume all responsibility for display and sale of merchandise.
The shop will be responsible for all losses due to theft, shoplifting and damage.
The Supplier will receive 50% of the price of all merchandise sold
and the Shop will retain 50%.
The Shop will issue to the Supplier a check for their percentage of the sales at the end of each month. The Shop will provide all necessary accounting and forms for records.
Either party may cancel this agreement with a 30 day written notice.

Supplier_____ Date_____
Shop _____ Date_____

Original/Shop   *Copy/Vendor*

CONSIGNMENT CONTRACT #1

Date _____

Gift Shop_____

Address _____

_____

Phone _____

Consignor_____

Address _____

_____

Phone _____

The items listed below are hereby consigned by consignor_____
for sale in the _____shop, referred to as the consignee.
The commission for displaying marketing and selling these items will be
_____% to the consignee. The consignor will receive _____%.
Payment to the consignor for the items sold will be at the conclusion of each month and not
more than 30 days after sale.
Consignee agrees to pay consignor the agreed percentage for any loss due to negligence, fire
or theft. All items that do not sell within 120 days will be returned to the consignor in good
condition.

ITEM#	DESCRIPTION	Quantity	Consignors %	Consignees %	Retail Price

TOTALS_____

Signed_____Consignee_____Consignor

Original/Consignee   Copy/Consignor

CONSIGNMENT CONTRACT #2

Consignment Sales Agreement

Supplier referred to as the Consignor of merchandise, and Gift Shop or Merchant referred to as consignee.

The consignor_____ consigns to the
consignee_____ the following goods:

_____

_____

_____

_____

Consignor may recall and take possession of the consigned property at any time.

Consignment Merchant (Consignee) shall sell the consigned property at a price not below the cost to the Consignor. As compensation for the sale made Consignee shall receive a commission of _____%

Consignee shall provide a verified accounting, every thirty days to Consignor, accompanied by payment in full for percentage of consigned property sold during the thirty-day period.

All consigned property shall be returned in good condition, to the Consignor after a _____day period. Cost for returning item shall be paid by the Consignor.

Dated: _____

_____
Consignor

_____
Consignee

_____
Name of Shop

Original/Consignee-Shop   Copy/Consignor-Supplier

EMPLOYEE PAYROLL DEDUCTION CONTRACT

Date: _____

Employee Name: _____

Department: _____

Extension #: _____

Home Address: _____

_____

Home Phone _____

Merchandise

Purchased: _____

_____

_____

_____

Total Amount of Purchase: $_____

Amount to be deducted monthly: $ _____ 25% of total

I authorize _____ to deduct the above amount from my payroll check each pay period, starting on _____ until the above total amount is paid in full. I further authorize _____, in the event of my termination, to apply my final payroll check towards my indebtedness, in accordance with Federal regulations. I agree to pay any remaining balance.

I have possession of the above merchandise.

_____

Shop Attendant's Signature

_____

Employee's Signature

Coded on _____ by_____

3-page form: Original- Accounting 1st Copy - Shop   2nd Copy – Employee

LAY-A-WAY CONTRACT

Lay-a-way #_____

Date: _____

Shop Name: _____

Address: _____

_____

Phone: _____

Customer: _____

Address: _____

_____

Phone: _____

Description of Merchandise: Price

_____

_____

_____

_____

       Tax   _____

       Total   _____

       Deposit (25%) _____

       Balance owed _____

I agree to make weekly___ monthly ___payments of $_____, paying off the balance by
_____, 20__. I understand that the merchandise will be returned to stock and that I will
forfeit the money already paid, if merchandise is not claimed and paid for by this date.
Customer's Signature: _____

Payment Record

Date   Received by Amount Paid   Balance Due

_____

_____

_____

_____

LAY-A-WAY #_____

NAME _____

PHONE _____

PICK UP DATE _____

2 page form with tear off label to attach to merchandise
Top copy to Customer - Bottom copy in Shop

Returned Check - 1st Letter

_____, 200__

Dear _____,

The bank has returned your check # _____ in the amount of
$ _____ payable to _____, for insufficient funds.

Enclosed is a copy of the bank statement showing a fee of $_____for this transaction.

I know that you will want to take care of this as soon as possible.

Please bring cash or money order in the amount of $_____
($_____, the amount of purchase and $_____for the bank charge) to the Gift Shop.

The posted Gift Shop fee of $_____, for returned checks, will be waived if the money is returned to the Gift Shop with-in two business days of receipt of this letter.

_____, Manager

Returned Check - 2nd Letter

_____, 200_

Re: Returned check # _____

Dear

Your check dated _____, in the amount of $_____ given in payment for merchandise from the _____ Gift Shop has been returned by the bank marked _____.

Amount of returned check $ _____
Returned check charge $ _____
Gift Shop Charge $ _____
Total due $ _____

You have seven (7) business days from receipt of this letter to send or bring payment in the form of cash, cashier's check or money order, for the total due, to the Gift Shop, or this matter will automatically be referred to the _____ County Attorney for prosecution.

_____,
Manager
Gift Shop

RECEIPT FOR COLLECTION OF RETURNED CHECKS

Date_____, 200__

Check #_____

Name_____

Amount of Check $_____
Bank Fee $_____
Gift Shop Fee $_____

TOTAL DUE $_____
(cash, cashier's check or money order only)

Received by_____

Inventory Form

Type of Inventory ___ _____ **Page** ____ **of** _____

Item #	Description	Retail Price	Quantity	Cost	Extension

*Page Total*_____

Previous Page Total _____

*TOTAL*_____

INCOME STATEMENT

Revenues
    Gross sales   _____
        Sales returns and allowances   _____
        Sales discounts   _____
    Net sales   _____
Cost of goods sold
    Beginning inventory (1/1)   _____
        Merchandise purchases   _____
        Freight   _____
    Net purchases   _____
    Cost of Goods available for sale _____
        Ending inventory (12/31)   _____
    Cost of Goods sold   _____
Gross profit   _____
Operating expenses
    Selling expenses
        Salaries for Part-Time Sales   _____
        Advertising   _____
        Supplies   _____
        Phone   _____
        Equipment   _____

                                     _____
        Miscellaneous   _____
        Sales Tax Expense   _____

    Total expenses   _____

Net income   _____

Balance Sheet

Assets
    Current assets
        Cash   _____
        Inventory   _____
        Supplies   _____

        Total current assets   _____
    Fixed assets
        Equipment
            Less: Accumulated depreciation   _____
        Business Machinnes   _____
            Less: Accumulated depreciation   _____
        Furniture and fixtures   _____
            Less: Accumulated depreciation   _____

        Total fixed assets   _____

Intangible assets
    Goodwill
        Total intangible assets   _____
    Total assets   _____

Liabilities
    Current liabilities
        Accounts payable   _____
        State Tax   _____
        Accrued salaries(if applicable)   _____

        Total current liabilities   _____

Total liabilities   _____

        RETAINED EARNINGS   _____

Shoplifting is Stealing!

It is not a prank, joke or thrill.

It is a Crime!

You could be punished with up to **$2000**
in fines and **5 or more years**
in prison, plus a record that will
haunt you for the rest of your life!

We prosecute shoplifters!

QUESTIONS? NEED HELP? BULK ORDERS?

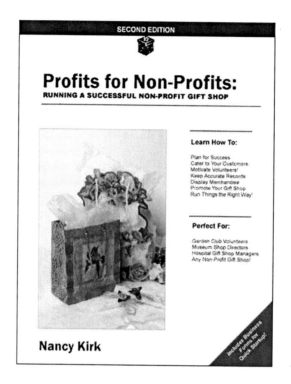

Feel free to email Nancy Kirk, nancykirk@houston.rr.com, with any questions, comments or suggestions. Or visit www.giftshopguide.com for more tips or information.

This book is available for quantity discounts for orders of 10 or more.

Contact ExpandingPress @ info@expandingpress.com or contact the author directly.

ISBN 1-4116-0518-7

Copyright 2005 & 2006 Nancy Kirk

http://www.giftshopguide.com